Looking
Back
with
Hack

Looking Back with Hack

HACK MILLER

DESERET NEWS
PUBLISHING CO.

ISBN 0-88494-432-8

First Printing, 1981

Lithographed in the United States of America
PUBLISHERS PRESS
Salt Lake City, Utah

Contents

Put It Back, Harold

There are skeletons in everyone's closet. Let me tell you about my closet, for instance.

My young years were spent in South Salt Lake, along the banks of Mill Creek. In the 1920s this was a clear-water stream. Dad used to come home from work, pick up his fly rod, and go to the stream for a little evening fly fishing.

We lived on Gregson Avenue, near Second East Street. Dad would fish downstream to State Street and sometimes fish the big hole where the water came out of the Hustler Mill chute. It was an interesting stretch of water. Watercress formed long the edges of the stream, and this cress was habitat for the small fresh-water shrimp.

One fisherman, most every day, would debark from the State Street streetcar, put on his fishing boots, and creel and fish up the creek to Second East and then fish back to State Street. Ceremoniously he would catch some shrimp in a cheesecloth net he had fashioned for such a purpose. Never did he fail to catch enough fish for dinner — about half a dozen nice rainbows each trip.

He was outfitted like a city dude, so we kids thought. Never had we seen anyone with a special creel like he had, a bait can that fit on his belt, a split bamboo fishing pool. This guy was someone! And to come on the streetcar at four cents each way — he had to have money, and he surely could afford to buy whatever fish he needed to eat. But we admired him for his tenacity at the sport he seemed to enjoy so much.

And I learned much from him. I chanced by him several

times, and in true Izaak Walton manner he would talk to me and show me how he threaded his shrimp. He used a small hook — unlike the huge anchor we used. Our equipment was like a tow hook and cable compared to his.

He had fine catgut leader material, and one day gave me some. That's when I learned to fish nymph-style — with the subterranean baits.

In the next few years I learned to thread a shrimp daintily, lead it with a B-B sinker, and let it drift in the currents down the clear-water runways alongside the watercress. And I learned to set the hook at the lightest bite.

We didn't have transportation restrictions in those days. If you caught a fish, you could bucket it and take it home for the goldfish bowl or whatever you wanted to do with it.

I built a cement fish pond at home near where Dad had put a water pipe to the front lawn. I tapped the pipe and put in a spray that kept the water fresh. Day by day I added a few Mill Creek trout to my pond, and soon had thirty-six fish as my pets. The grasshopper crop was just right, so feed was easy to get — even though Mother didn't like my beating the fields with her new flyswatter.

The worst part of this operation was that I got too friendly with my fish and had to catch new ones each time we had trout for supper. I couldn't kill my thirty-six little friends which I was hand-feeding daily.

That problem was solved quickly one day. My brother, Eldon, caught a huge carp and thought my trout ought to have some big play pals, so he put the carp in the pond. Next morning all but eight of the trout were on the ground around the pond. I never did conclude just what happened in that carp-trout skirmish.

Even in those days the fishing season didn't open until about mid-June. That was a long time for kids to wait along the banks of Mill Creek. By then we were swimming in the big hole we had dug at the end of Nelson's Grove, complete with diving board. We had already begun our pollywog collection from our frog ponds, and some of them we would use for bait for the big fish near the swimming holes. We had fashioned some rafts and small boats for the many runs we would make between Third East and State Street. Some of these were tar and canvas — when we could find some old road tar to cook up for the sealer. Crude they were, but they floated. We had watched the fish feed the surface of the stream as we swung, Tarzan-like, on the ropes that hung from the Nelson Grove trees.

In Nate Pearce's field we set up jumping pits for high jumps. We were aspiring athletes in those days. We had a discus and made a discus ring. Lee Warburton had the use of a football. His brother, Bub, played quarterback for Utah Aggies and had a football on loan to keep his passing arm sharp. We kept that football busy, and as it turned out that old Aggie football saw a lot of service with such greats-to-be as Turk Jackson, Bob Bunker, and Ken Shell.

We were all playing in the Pearce plot one spring when someone suggested setting a line or two down the muskrat hole at the river's bend — maybe catching a few fish. After all, the season would open in one week, and there would be plenty of fish for everyone.

We had one problem. Bill Bingley was the game warden, and occasionally he would station himself in the loft of the Hustler Flour Mill between State Street and what was later to become Main Street. He could see the creek for a mile in either direction. Bill had spy glasses, as we called them, to watch for people who broke the law.

Bill Bingley had a wooden leg and couldn't run very fast — and he couldn't swim because his leg would get water-logged. He was one of the finest conservation officers the state ever had. Kids never had a better friend than he was. I came to know Bill well in the years that followed. I never did ask him about his wooden leg.

It was only thirty-five yards from the river's bend to the cow barn where we hung our fishing rods for the winter, mostly bamboo poles about ten or twelve feet long, with wire guides and two-bit reels on them. Our fishing line was mostly kite string. Our plan was to play touch football, and when a man was tackled he would lie on the ground and reach into one of the muskrat holes and check our set lines. Then if Bill was watching us he would think we were just frolicking with the football.

One of the football fishermen got a big bite, and we tried hard to cover the landing of a five-pound brown trout — the largest fish we had ever seen in Mill Creek since my Mother, on opening day two years earlier, had caught a six-pounder. We kept in the grass, and finally one of the kids made a dash for it to the barn — where we had a tub of water near the artesian well. The fish liked that water, and in a short time we were through with football. We were looking at the biggest fish we had ever seen.

The Jacksons on Thirty-third South and Main Street operated a service station. Turk had to take the fish home to show everyone at the station. The tub held the fish adequately. No fuss with the fish. We displayed it, keeping silent on our illegal adventure.

When Dad came home that night the fish was swimming around in our bathtub. "Where did you get it?" he asked.

"From the Creek," I said, in pure George Washington cherry-tree fashion.

From that moment I hedged a little. I couldn't tell an old trouter like my Dad the fish just swam ashore and we were saving it from that fate. Nor would he believe that it had run up the Nelson ditch on a spawning lark and got trapped in the irrigation weir.

"You've got to put the fish back, Harold," my Dad decreed. He wasn't mad. Maybe he was glad to know just where the fish came from — the bend in the river.

And maybe this is the reason that on opening day he was there an hour before 4:00 A.M. opening, stationed in the right spot to take the big one if the fish wanted to bite again.

And I was right there with him. And so were Turk and Lee and some others who had heard about the big fish at the Jackson Service Station.

Harold did return the fish to Mill Creek. And they never saw each other again. That opening day no one caught the big brown trout. But its memory lingered with us during all the years we lived there.

I told Bill Bingley about it several years later — how we kids had borrowed one of his fish for an afternoon.

He smiled. He knew his young friends had learned a lesson.

Governor Misses His "Buck"

Governor J. Bracken Lee was one of the best sportsmen I ever knew. He was a sharpshooter with the skeet and trap gun. He could fish and fell fowl with the best of them. In fact, his lovely lady told me once that they spent their honeymoon in a tent in one of the drainage canyons of the Uinta Forest. And that's being a fisherman in anyone's book.

He was sitting on the steps of the governor's mansion when I arrived at 3:00 A.M. He had cleared all affairs of state for this one day — this was his day to go afield and see if the laws he had signed anent fishing and hunting matters were appropriately made.

Our destination was Chalk Creek, up Weber Canyon from Morgan. We were to hunt the Dearden property, which I knew very well. I also had the two best deer-hunting guides in the known world to help me find the governor a target or two. These were Alva Dearden, who had the key to the gate, and Rulon Francis, who was so much a part of the landscape in that area he never needed anyone's key. I always claimed he

In a pre-hunt huddle, Governor J. Bracken Lee second from left.

knew the deer and their habits so well that he, like a Tarzan, might have been raised by a deer herd.

We hunted hard that day and the governor did get some shooting — long shots some of them — two boxes' worth. He claimed he didn't kill this one nice buck, but we were sure he did. His sportsmanship was showing. So we looked for another whereon he could attach his tag.

The setting sun was closing out our day and we elected to get in the truck and patrol the high ridges. This was the way to hunt the back country both at sunrise and sunset — the deer would at that time be on the browse, and the browse was on the open slopes and ridges.

As we moved along the ridge between Coal Hollow and Francis Canyon we saw a nice buck bounding toward us on the shade side of the ridge. Now and then, as it bounced through the brush, the sun would glisten on its antlers.

Someone had spooked it.

We stopped the truck, got aground, and then watched the buck take cover in a patch of oak brush. But we had it covered, so we thought.

About ten seconds after the buckskin bounced into the brush we saw another animal come out of it. Naturally we thought it was the same buck. We yelled to the governor that the deer was coming over the ridge.

But that wasn't the buck at all. The buck had spooked a large doe deer out and over the hump — while the buck slipped off down the small ravine to the bottom of the canyon. We didn't know this until we looked for the buck later and saw it bounding far down the canyon, out of range.

Yell as we did that the buck was coming into view, the governor had to take a look at it before he pulled the trigger. About to shoot, he saw no "horns" and he unshouldered his gun and let the deer pass. Beautiful doe, it was. Governor Lee gave a big sigh. He was glad he had held his fire.

We didn't get another shot on that ridge, but down the canyon the governor was able to hang his tag on a nice four-point buck. We cleaned it quickly and were soon out of the canyon with a handsome display of mule deer. It was a day the governor will never forget.

At the checking station near Morgan we stopped for inspection. Wardens there were glad their big boss had been on a hunt, had seen what some of the problems were. While some of the sportsmen were chatting with Governor Lee the inspecting warden came and whispered to me, "Has the governor got another tag? He has last year's tag on his deer." I took Bracken Lee aside and asked him to get the other tag from his wallet, which he did. We just added another tag.

There's this to say for the governor: He bought a fishing and hunting license every year, whether or not he fished or hunted. That was his way of participating in the upkeep of the resource. He must have had drawers full of unused deer tags. He could have tied thirteen tags, at least, to that deer.

Next day I saw Governor Lee on Main Street and we talked about the events of the day before. "Say," he said, "It's a good thing we spotted that doe in time, or I could have been arrested and gone to jail."

What can you say when part of his scare was your fault? You chuckle it off, as I did right then, with, "Well, there would have been three of us to share the time in the hoosegow with you. We told you to shoot it!"

Another time we were fishing with Governor J. Bracken Lee. Felix Koziol, Chet Olsen, Larry Colton, Wes Hamilton and I had taken Governor Lee into the Amethyst Lake country on the north side of Hayden Peak. It was a horseback ride of eight or ten miles — into some of the state's most beautiful country. You get there up the Stillwater Country, Christmas Meadows — south of Evanston, Wyoming.

Bracken Lee mentioned he was no horseman — only because he hadn't sat in the saddle for too many seasons. So we shaped him with the softest saddle we had, gave him the horse with the best gait and the one which was thinnest at its withers.

We got to the lake area and established camp. Then we went fishing. Brack limped a little and never sat on a rock. Even while eating dinner that night he leaned against a tree. No doubt he was hurting near the hind pockets — and we were hurting for him.

Next day Larry suggested we ride around and find the lake with the best fishing. A sheepherder in a nearby camp told us where the biggest fish were — a small lake hidden in a glacier-cut canyon. It wasn't much of a ride, but on each sortie Brack insisted on walking his horse. He and his horse walked a lot of miles in the next few days.

Came the time when we had to pull stakes and go down the canyon. We conferenced about saddles — to be sure he had the one that would fit Brack best, leg length for the stirrups considered.

Going down canyon is always harder on your legs than riding up the hills. You fight the saddle rather than sit in it. You strain to keep from sliding over the horn onto the horse's neck. And Brack did just that — strained with every step the horse took down the steep trail.

It was smooth in the meadowlands and this gave Bracken some smooth-saddle time. But at the horse trailers we noted that Brack couldn't slide out of the saddle. He had been soldered to it. Sheer grit couldn't move him. He tried and tried again. Finally two of us lifted him by the arms while a third led his horse from under him. Rigor mortis had set in, Brack admitted, in certain parts of his anatomy.

Going home we slowed for every road rut, and no matter how easy we went he flinched every time.

Over the years we have had our load of laughs about how sore he was that day. And he never lost his love for horses. But you never caught him leading any of the Pioneer Day parades on someone's palomino.

Bracken Lee never took much of the state's fish and game in all his days. But I learned later that he had his deer duly processed and donated it to the inmates of the Utah State Prison. Sometimes what few fish he caught went to the same place.

One other governor joined me in an outdoor venture. George Dewey Clyde, one of the finest men I ever knew, had just signed the life-jacket law into effect. That required children under twelve to wear life jackets at all times while in a boat, and others to have the necessary number of jackets readily available in the boat, if not worn. It was a controversial law for a while, in spite of some unnecessary loss of lives in storms when boats were capsized and life jackets were not worn.

Governor Clyde had accepted my invitation to go to Panguitch Lake for the opening day. The lake had been treated several years before and a new strain of trout was ready to be harvested. We wanted to show the governor the wonderful effect of the state's treatment program. John Talmage, the governor's assistant and an old newspaper crony of many years, joined us.

Everyone else in the state figured Panguitch Lake was the place to be. There were so many boats on the lake when we went to the dock early that morning, before daylight (we wanted to let out the first trolling line exactly at 4:00 A.M.), we could hardly make our way to our craft.

We waited our turn to unlash the boat and go onto the lake. Then John remembered we had a new life-jacket law and suggested that, in view of the trafficked condition, the governor wear his jacket.

With his coat on to prevent getting chilled, it was not easy to fit the governor. He was a big man, and we had to loosen many straps to get them around him. He was overpadded for this occasion and showed some resentment about the jackets.

"You mean to say I signed that law?" he said to John.

John meant to say that.

"That's silly," Governor Clyde quipped with a smile. "If you fell out of a boat here you would have to fall into someone else's."

And that was about the way Panguitch opening was that year — boat to boat, where one oar was always knocking against another boat.

We caught fish, some nice ones.

Later in the day we decided to fish with flies. I never have worn a hard hat while fishing. In fairness to both John and Governor Clyde, I never knew worse fly fishermen. With three in a boat, the fly hooks were buzzing around us like a swarm of bees forming on a wild pear tree. I gave up fly fishing and took to ducking and netting what dumb trout took their flies.

After a hook or two glanced off the governor's jacket, I suggested a remedy: we would troll our flies at very slow speed — try the unusual trick. With two lines out we had a pleasant time trolling flies and caught some nice fish — enough for the governor and John to take home some rainbow fillets.

I've trolled a lot of flies for lake trout. That was the first time I did it in self-defense.

Get Close to the Moss

Happenstance is fishing's best tutor. If it happens, you learn about it. Like fly fishing the moss lanes in September.

The lake was heavy with moss. Charley Woodbury said that he had had some good fishing against the gravel banks at the west side of the lake, between where the Strawberry River enters the lake and Clark's camp.

Dr. John Dixon, Daryl Shumway and I asked Charley's advice and then took it. We anchored about three hundred yards from the shoreline, in a likely place where we could miss the moss by casting in several directions.

Shumway was famous for his nighttime fly fishing. This midday antic was not his angle. In fact, he knew so little about it he had his two rods in the boat, both of them outfitted with last fall's flies, the water still in the bubble. He had us fooled, if he knew anything about daytime fishing.

I was still anchoring the boat when he made a first cast. The rod bent as he grunted. I was bent over, but I looked up to see the action on the tip of the rod. He was tied into a tonner, so it seemed.

John Dixon was quick to cast his flies, and before Shumway had his fish boatside Dixon was tied into one. We had come at feeding time, found the right spot, with the right flies and were into the fish. Boaters from miles around began to pull anchor. We would soon have company. We knew that.

We were in a prime spot on the lake, laned out in the moss. As anxious as other fishermen were to come in close to us, they could not. The moss managed their movements this time. They watched from other spots where they could motor to open water.

Dixon and Shumway were both fighting their fish — or the fish were fighting them.

"Get the net," Shumway said.

Net? I never had a boat net. I figured that whatever fish I

wanted in my boat I could lift them in, either on the line or by gilling them gently at the boat's gunwales.

We didn't lose a fish, sans net.

Shumway had broken all the Strawberry rules, mostly rules he had made himself. In midday the big fish would not take the big skunk-tailed streamers. These were night flies. But Daryl hadn't taken a moment to take the streamers off his leader. No way would he use streamers of this size on the midday moss lanes at the Strawberry Reservoir.

But catching fish is different. The rules changed that day.

When I saw what was happening, I jerked the daytime flies from my leaders and tied up with the black and red devil flies, as the skunk-hairs are called.

It was twenty minutes to one in the afternoon. This is the time when the worm witchers and marshmallow floaters bait up and let their baits work for them while fishermen take their naps.

Dixon and Shumway had fish on so fast I couldn't get a line in the water for hoisting their fish aboard. That was the penalty for my not having a net for them to use. They had boated seven beautiful cutthroats and rainbow trout before I got a strike.

I learned another lesson right then. I had been field-testing some line for one of the manufacturers, and I decided then that the fluorescent lines were not made for the clear waters at the Strawberry. I changed leaders pronto. First cast with the plain, clear leader and I was tied into a nice trout.

It was Shumway who suggested I was using the wrong leader material. This was expensive stuff — about three dollars a spool. He loaned me some sixty-nine-cent material and that turned the trick.

Incidentally, I wrote to my friend who manufactured the colored line and told him my story. It made no matter; they made a fortune selling the fluorescent stuff to us fishermen.

It could be that the leader was not the cause of my distress. Maybe my luck hadn't turned as yet in my favor. But I shall never think that changing the colored leader for the plain monofilament line did not make the difference that day. For sure, I was not going to believe in my failure to the extent that I would spend a pleasant day on the lake, lifting other fellows' fish into the boat.

On one cast and retrieve Shumway had both Dixon and Miller with their heads over the gunwhale of the boat. He had two fish on and was having more tussle than one fish can ever offer. He needed help.

Both fish were cutthroats, and that astounded us. When he first got his strike we watched a silvery rainbow of about four pounds shoot into the sky — like a swordfish at LaPaz. Now he had two native trout boatside. Obviously, the rainbow had thrown the hook, and in the retrieving process two cutthroats had invited themselves to lunch at Shumway's table.

Three fish on one cast. We got two of them in the boat. That is when we needed the net.

That was the prettiest catch of seventeen trout I had ever seen. We fished no more than an hour and a half.

We had hardly pulled anchor when two loads of fishermen came in upon us — to take our place. They also wanted to know what we were using. That was as important as having the hole.

They didn't believe what we told them, so it made little difference. Streamer flies of that size during the heat of the day! We must have been kidding them, so they reasoned. We didn't linger long enough to prove any points. We told the truth and left the lake.

That day I learned much about fishing, to wit:

Don't go by all the rules — especially those rules you have made yourself.

When someone says it won't work, try it!

And don't believe everything you read on the packages sold in the fishing stores. The guy who wrote those tidbits of information about fishing and how to use the product attached never anchored in a lane of moss on a September day on Strawberry Reservoir.

As for me, I have stocked up on that old-fashioned clear monofilament leader material — that fifty-cent stuff!

Now Where Did That Buck Go?

It could only happen to an old-timer like Wayne Murdock of Heber.

Wayne has fee title to many thousands of acres in the rangelands east of Strawberry Reservoir. He has hunted that land since the time he was old enough to halter a horse — long before he could set a saddle on a Morgan mare.

He knows every hill and vale, where every deer can hide, where the bucks will break out of the brush. He knows where to be whenever there are other hunters in the area. I have hunted a few years with Wayne, and no one knows the deer and their doings any better than he does.

One day, with his wife, Chris, he trucked over a ridge and waited, as he had done many times before. A hunter's waiting sometimes worries the deer and, as bucks will do, sometimes they grow curious and appear when they shouldn't.

A big buck did that for Wayne and Chris as they watched from a high spot at a favorite basin where the monarchs seemed to hide after they had been hunted heavily in the back country.

The grass was deep this hunt in that particular draw. It was deep enough to hide a deer if the animal elected to hole up and wait it out.

Maybe it was the sudden calm that got the big deer on his legs. It stood there in the grass like a giraffe in the Transvaal country of South Africa. Big!

This was the buck Wayne wanted on this hunt. He was an excellent shot, and he picked his target spot. The deer slumped in the grass and Wayne and Chris motored off the mountain, down a dugway and then leveled their truck out in the tall grass. It was a bumpy ride — just the way Wayne Murdock liked it.

He got his knife from the rack of the truck, and took some cloths with him. At preparing a deer no one could beat him.

But the deer was not to be found. He beat the brush as Chris remained in the cab of the truck. Half an hour passed, and Wayne had wandered all around looking for a spot where his buck might have bled or broken out of the basin.

He came back and sat in the truck.

"I did shoot a deer," he said to Chris. "It did fall down."

He shook his head. What next?

"Have you looked under the truck?" Chris asked.

At this point, as Wayne told us the story several days later, he was too chagrined to look in that spot. He was very much concerned that the buck would be there and the last laugh would be on him.

It was there.

Every hunt since then Wayne's friends have brought that matter to his attention.

"Have you looked under the truck?"

"If you shoot at anything today, be sure and look under the truck."

I realized that Wayne had come of age with his own story when, on the last time we hunted his mountains, he chuckled and reminded us, "And be sure and look under the truck."

And we always do.

The Strawberry Reservoir

If there is a better trout fishing water in the world than Utah's Strawberry Reservoir, patronage considered, I would like to find it.

But then a lake like the Strawberry can't be everyone's best lake. One must learn how to make it the best lake — learn its tricks. The lake is a jealous mistress, and if you're going to love the old gal you have to spend some time learning her wants and ways.

I have worked diligently over the seasons to solve some of the Strawberry riddles. It is intriguing in every respect. You can catch the big fish one night and never get a nibble the next day.

Some days you feel the lake is almost human. It is loving and kind, like a lady can be. Then it can be wretched and wild, like a lady can be.

In your romance with the lake you often have a desire to keep your secrets to yourself. If the lady of the lake smiles lovingly on you, it is your fine fortune. Selfishly, you sometimes feel that anyone who wishes to know your success factors, on given days, is asking more than is polite — or even acceptable. It was like that the night several of us were fishing along the shores of Mud Bay near Clark's camp.

I was catching fish. So were Daryl Shumway, Wayne Murdock and Kenny Johnson, who were fishing with me, each posting himself so he could make some slant casts without intruding upon the other's domain. That's one of the tricks of fishing in the dark of the evening when the big fish swallow up to chase the minnows along the shoreline.

This particular night more fishermen were cruising the shoreline in their vehicles than were wading the icy waters of the lake. But I have never caught a fish sitting behind the car's hot-air flow. You have to get in the lake — or have a line in it.

In the dark of the night flashlights are necessary. You must know the area you are wading — or you might fall in, as I did one November twenty-eighth at 8:50 P.M., over my head. The ice was forming all around us that night. It was cold. And I was clumsy!

Also, you must use lights to check your lures — to be sure the leader is not tangled. You must constantly check fly hooks for moss or other debris.

When you are landing a fish you need a light to be sure you get the fish on the shore — sometimes over a shelf of ice which forms hard around the lake's edge, created by the waves of the day's storms.

Some cars were stopped along the dirt road to our backs as we landed a couple of nice native trout. Jealously, we guarded our spots by showing as little light as possible. The way we fished, spaced adequately to allow fan casting, we could not crowd the other fishermen. Each respected the other's "fishing hole."

As I landed a fifth fish I didn't notice a man standing behind me. He flashed his light squarely into my face. My eyes had become adjusted to the dark, and the bright light was a shocker for sure.

I showed my instant resentment at being flashed down.

"You Hack Miller?" he asked.

My answer was curt. Like President Herbert Hoover once said, "There are two times when a man should be left to himself — when he's fishing and when he's praying."

I'm a Hoover man in that respect.

"Who is Hack Miller?" I bluntly retorted.

"He's one who knows this lake pretty good, and I was told if I could find him I could find the fish — because he would be in them."

That was flattery, and I should have been gentler with the gentleman. But there was no room around for another fisherman. I avoided the handshaking and all those nice American social customs and went on fishing. He scanned my catch of big trout with his flashlight.

"Seems you don't need Hack Miller," he said, and he left.

This was a night of visitors. The next man came up and focused his light on my flies as I checked the lures for moss.

"You're using Shumway's flies," he said.

Of course I was. Daryl Shumway, one of the world's best fly-tying Strawberry fishermen, was fishing just fifty yards away. Daryl listened to the whole conversation. So many anglers knew Daryl and tried to follow him around the rim of the lake when Shumway was snagging the big fish, that we talked in parables. I called him Ralph. He called me Nathan, or Harold. I preferred him to use Nathan because my mother named me Harold.

The visitor knew Shumway's flies when he saw them. They were available at most every good store in Heber and at the self-service gas station on the southwest side of town.

"I am?" I replied in surprise.

"Who's Shumway?" I asked quickly, loud enough to let Shumway hear our conversation.

"He's a good fisherman and the only one who ties most of his flies with the jungle-cock eye." he said.

"I'm glad to know that. I bought these when I got gas at the service station and didn't know whether they would catch a fish or not. They seem to work."

I kept fishing while the man, standing in the dark and flashing his light on the fish I had lying in the snow, kept talking. That was all right, except that next cast I tied into a lunker rainbow that kept trying to get himself into the air. I kept a low rod, hoping to hide the success I was having. I let the fish play as long as he wanted, hoping, by the second, that my visitor would get the heck on his way.

You can't keep a dancing rainbow trout a secret from shoreline bystanders.

I might have showed my bad side when I suggested, "I would ask you to stay and fish with us, but we're spaced about as tight as fishing will allow." Sporting man that he was, he noted what fly I caught that last rainbow on and left.

The fish was a beautiful hybrid buck (native-rainbow cross). It was as silver as a show saddle in the flashlight beam.

The fly patterns are important, but Bill Ewer, a colleague at the *Deseret News* for many years, proved one night, at this same Mud Creek shoreline, that you don't have to have the skunk-hairs and the jungle-cock cheeks on a fly to take the night feeders.

Bill just held his spot at Mud Creek Bay, kept casting the patterns usually used for the daytime, and caught more fish than some of us with the fancy flies we had concocted — which we contended were the best for night fishing. Sometimes the best is not that good.

Bill contended, and rightfully so, that patience is a virtue in fishing the Strawberry Reservoir at night. "Just wait them out. They will come into the shoreline to feed and they will take most any good pattern in flies," Bill said.

But there is a technique on which most of the experts agree. In fishing bubble and flies on a spinning rod, fill the bubble with about a thumbnail of air — so it just rides beneath the lake's surface. Retrieve the flies slowly, holding the rod high to detect the slightest "bite." The fish "mouth" the flies rather than strike them.

At such a slow retrieve an angler must be able to set the hook. That is the trick of it.

You've Killed My Bait

It was January in 1958, out of the baseball season, when Chuck Dressen, manager of the Dodgers, found a little fishing time and accepted an invitation from a friend named Jimmy Schuyler of Las Vegas to go fishing on Lake Mead.

The Thunderbird Hotel, where Jimmy was one of the

bosses, maintained a nice fishing-sporting boat at the Lake. Jimmy, knowing that I was in daily need of a sports column for my newspaper, asked me and my wife to go along. Also, over the years, I had been friend of Jim's, and whenever we met in Las Vegas we spent a little time together. He was a great source of sporting information — a fine sport himself.

We had talked about a fishing trip on Lake Mead many times. When he invited Chuck and Ruth Dressen to go on the lake he included Barbara and me.

Now, Barbara and Ruth were not fisher ladies, or whatever they call them (maybe fisher-persons). They liked the ride on the beautiful lake and more or less agreed, on their own initiative, to stay out of the fishermen's way.

Chuck Dessen was a devoted man in many ways. He loved his wife, maybe less than he loved baseball. But Ruth, in explaining his love for baseball, confessed that if her hubby liked her second to baseball that was the most anyone could possibly be loved by a husband.

Ruth chuckled as she told how, during the "off" season, Chuck would get up in the morning, take the baseball cap from the night-stand, don it for the day, and then go to breakfast in his Dodger shirt. He wore his spikes if he walked around the yard after breakfast.

It was a spectacular January day as we cruised from the docking area near Henderson to take up fishing position along some favorite shoreline shoals where the boatmen knew the best fishing to be. Chuck preferred to plug the shoreline before he turned to using the live baits. Plugging, as Chuck and Jimmy knew, was much more sporting. But if the plugs didn't produce, there was always the vat of salamanders which the boatmen kept ready for the hotel's guest fishermen.

A few moves with the plugs, and Chuck turned to the salamanders — or "waterdogs" as the lake's fishermen called them. Chuck elected to choose his own bait, and as he dipped into the live-bait vat he grabbed a waterdog as long as his fungo bat — eight inches at least. I wondered what bigmouth bass would attempt to attack such a monster. But the boatmen assured Chuck that big bait always brings big fish. Chuck was going for the four-ply slammer. He didn't want any bunts and singles this day. Go for the big one!

Jimmy hooked the bait for Chuck — deep in the lips so it would stand the heavy cast. Chuck was fishing with a Mitchell, open-faced reel, and he admitted several times while he was plug casting that this was not his favorite gear. But he seemed to be getting the "hang" of it with the plugs, and no one paid him any heed.

With the big bait bending his long rod, he swung the salamander back for the long cast. Then something went wrong. The bale of the reel flipped back and stayed the line. The salamander turned into a whiplash and caught my wife, who was standing several feet away at what she considered safe distance, flush to the side of her head.

Barbara staggered and then leaned against the cabin. Chuck was mortified — he stood in a freeze.

For Barbara the birds were singing and the stars were sparking. Gene Fullmer never took a better blow to the belfry. All the bells were ringing, Barbara explained later.

What could Chuck say? He quickly put the rod down, and when he saw Barbara's eyes straighten from the crossed position and an embarrassed smile spring to her face, he did the best he could. "Look, Mrs. Miller," he said pointing to the lifeless waterdog on the deck. "You've killed my bait."

We laughed that off right then, Barbara assuring Chuck that she was all right — that the fish was rather a flabby one to be placed against a rather hard head. We laughed about the incident many times during that pleasant day. No headache for milady.

That day was a pleasant one with the Dressens and Jimmy Schuyler. And after being with such gentle people I have wondered often how a little guy like Chuck, a gentle person, could stand, as he often did, at home base and take on those great big umpires on a call that Chuck questioned.

The Moose Have the Right-of-way

It was on Henry's Fork of the Snake River. Sid Eliason and I were fishing from Big Springs to Mack's Inn in one boat, and Max Lewis and Lew Ellsworth were in another.

We launched our boats just downstream from Big Springs, where the big fish are fed by the tourists — with bread crumbs, popcorn, anything. And we wanted to fish as close to the "no fishing" signs as we could — hoping to get into one of those five-pound rainbows which might have strayed too far downstream. We actually hooked two of them as we went under the railroad trestle. Both of them just hit the lures as if they were feeding on popcorn at the bridge above. That, at least, started the day's fun for Sid and me. Lew and Max had gone on ahead.

We drifted leisurely to a spot Sid called the bathtub hole. We tied to the shoreline and then tried to determine what the fish wanted most, starting with lures. Now and then we felt the tug of a good fish, but with the water a little roily from the input from the Henry's Lake fork, we had to feel our fishing.

The wily rainbow trout hit a black flatfish best, but it took us some time to learn that trick. We went through most of the tackle box before we came upon a lure they liked.

First cast, Sid hooked into a whopper and was not ready for the action. The fish ran off with his flatfish. When I lost the only other flatfish we had of that hue, we decided we had underestimated the combativeness of these Henry's Fork fish. They appeared to be angry at something.

We caught some, one about three pounds. And we loitered in the hole until we figured we had offered the most we had and in the best effort. By this time there was a rain cloud coming overhead, with a black bottom, and we were urged to put afloat again and head downstream.

Around the bend in the river we suddenly changed our mind about floating very far. Five bull moose, a matched set of them, were feeding the river, snorkeling the grasses and reeds along the edges, wading dead center. And they appeared as if they intended to be there until it was time to shore up and chew cud.

Sid said the moose would move if I kept rowing toward them. But I took a good look at them and then looked for a tie-up. The rain started slowly — enough to wet a couple of fishermen if they stayed in their uncovered craft.

What is a man to do, a man who has been scared stiff of moose all his life, and grizzly bears and cobra snakes — the three most ferocious critters this fisherman could think of? No way was I going to bump the belly of a bull moose with my boat — with only a six-foot pine oar to fight with. Sid finally agreed with me; and that was comforting. I felt then like there were two cowards instead of just one.

We pulled the little rowboat to shore and turned it bottom up between two stumps. I kindled a small fire to take the chill off the world, broke open the lunch sack, and there we sat, in plain view of the five bull moose, hoping maybe they would take the hint and sportingly move on. Failing that, we hoped someone else would be floating the river and they would move the moose. So we waited.

Not until they had a bellyful of river reeds did the big bulls budge. Then we two cowards, bored of bending under a boat top in a miserable rain, put afloat and went our way.

Lew and Max wondered if they had left some great fishing, and as soon as we reached "port" they first examined our fishing creels. Had they blown the best part of the day by rushing ahead of the rain? This they had to know.

Well, they hadn't. Sid and I had half a dozen fish, one worth bragging about.

Nothing was said about the moose. Cowards never should confess their cowardice. Let it be, we decided, as we told how we could not leave the bathtub hole and how much fun we had had with so many fish that got away. Since that day I have never floated a river, waded a creek or taken water down an irrigation ditch without wondering what is around the next bend.

Flaming Gorge

In its first days, as.the waters were first collecting behind the Cart Creek Dam, Flaming Gorge Reservoir was the number one trout fishing spot in the known world. No place outside a hatchery was like it. While in those days there were no brown trout, no mackinaw, there were rainbows by the millions.

One day a California couple rented a boat from Bob Wetherspoon's Manila Marina. They returned in a couple hours without a fish. Bob was in a state of shock, and he immediately escorted them onto the lake. In half an hour he had them limited up with nice rainbow trout. Bob was not going to let anyone go from his place without a fishermen's smile on his face.

It seemed to all the experts at the time that the lake was overstocked with trout for the available feed the lake had. After all, this was merely backup water over an old sagebrush flat, the same flats that Butch Cassidy and his famous Wild Bunch likely roamed in their train-robbing days. A lake of this size would have to create a habitat for fish, so the scientists expected.

But that all made fishing superb, so the text books said. It was reasoned that the fish were always hungry because of the sparsity of natural feed. So they took whatever bait was offered them. Whatever the explanation, we fishermen liked our angling from that angle. Just keep those fish finding food, we contended.

The Green River, which supplied the Flaming Gorge water, was one of the famous brown trout rivers in the western world. The Green River headed at Green Lakes in Wyoming's Wind River Range, and from its beginning it was a brown trout stream.

When the two states, Utah and Wyoming, cooperated in preparing the Green River drainage for its role in creating Flaming Gorge Reservoir, the brown trout were killed. All of the river's tributaries were cleaned of existing fish, and only rainbow trout, so we were told at the time, were planted in the waters. But keeping the browns out of the brooks and rivers was impossible, and in due time they would return — which they did.

As time passed, the cannibalistic brown fed heartily upon the smaller rainbow, and soon the big chase was for brown. In time some huge fish were hung up for display. One of the first to attract national and international attention was the twenty-nine pounder caught by Verl Hanchett of Dutch John. The Hanchett fish was ten pounds lighter than the supposed world record listed for a Dr. Muir, caught in Scotland in 1866. The Muir fish was listed in the *Field and Stream* magazine records at thirty-nine pounds, eight ounces.

Fishermen soon turned their attention to the brown trout side of the lake. The experts were talking about a world record. As some of the biggies were boated, fishermen schooled themselves in how to fish for the browns. Whereas most fishermen had been using small lures, some flies, and the swill baits, the turn came to large flatfish, pop-gear and threaded minnows, Rapala baits — fish imitation lures of from six to ten inches.

And nighttime proved to be the best time to fish for the lunkers — they were on the prowl then. Some fishermen, gradually trying all tricks, found all-night fishing to be productive but cold and uncomfortable.

While the anglers were after their big browns they started

to catch sizeable mackinaw. Best fishing for the macks seem to be along the sandy points deep in the bay south of the Manila Marina, where much of the gravel was gathered in the building of the dam.

Hanchett's fish, incidentally, was the second largest brown trout caught in Utah's history. The biggest Beehive State brown was taken from a dam in Logan River drainage. It weighed thirty-six pounds, twelve ounces. There was some question about the legality of the Logan lunker, and *Field and Stream* magazine asked this writer to check up on that situation. Was it caught legally on rod and reel? Was it foul hooked? And so on.

Checking all sources I soon learned that the fish had been foulhooked, or netted, so it was not eligible for listing in the records. It did prove, though, that Utah had the record potential in brown trout.

Excitement grew at Flaming Gorge as all these records were reviewed. Could there be a fifty-pounder in the lake?

Experts reasoned there could be.

Pyramid Lake in Nevada had produced a record cutthroat at a time when the lake had been heavily stocked with smaller fish. Pyramid Lake also was in its first years, before the feed had been stabilized. Since those first years, although this lake has produced some fine fish, it has not come close to another record.

Lake Pend Oreille in Idaho was stocked with kamloop rainbow. The lake was famous for its nine-inch, blue-back salmon. The rainbows fed heartily upon the blue-backs, so we were told by those who were supposed to know, and in four years they had reached world record size — thirty-six pounds and larger. But as feed diminished in Lake Pend Oreille, so did the potbellies of the big kamloops.

Obviously this was the story of Flaming Gorge. The time will come, if the pattern holds, that the feed will reach a reasonable level and big fish will not be at record size. It takes a lot of small fish each day in a big fish diet to make a world record. When the big fish don't have a gluttonous gleaning they cease to grow to record size.

Some contend there might not be a forty-pounder in Flaming Gorge because of the stabilization situation.

Let's hope there is.

It Beats Haying the Horses

Some years before Flaming Gorge Reservoir was created behind the damsite at Dutch John and Cart Creek, I rode range with range management chiefs of the Utah Fish and Game Department and the Forest Service. By checking the range at the same time each spring, riding the same canyons and driving deer over the same flatlands, we could determine what the deer population was for that year in comparison with other years. And that had to be done to have proper management of the existing habitat. The Forest Service could also determine to what extent the public lands could be used for cattle and sheep grazing.

The first time I went along as one of the horsebackers and deer-counters I rode with Harold Crane, Casey Bown, Dick Bennett, Ernie Hirsch, and Bill Hurst. There was no bridge across the river at Manila. We checked the river ice for thickness and then rode horseback across that section of Antelope Flat to Bears Ear pass, down the canyon to Dutch John and to the state cabin, which was kept solely for game management purposes.

We picked our path carefully across the river ice. From the river it was a ten-mile ride to the base station.

The old cabin was cold when we arrived. Hay and grain had been stored for the horses. There were some chores to be done on the outside — getting the horses hayed and branned for the night. I was assigned to getting a fire going in the old coal stove, thawing out the cabin, warming up the bedding space and the sleeping bags, and cooking dinner. Steaks were the first order of business, so I was told.

I knew everyone was hungry. It had been a hard day since we sat beside a plate of hotcakes earlier in the day at Manila. So while the stove was heating and things were thawing out in general, I mixed a batch of baking powder biscuits. I added a few other ingredients, warmed the butter, got the honey runny.

When the hungry horde came in for a dash of hot washing water, they got a sniff at the cook's kitchenry, and one by one each snitched a biscuit. These were not the small dollar-sized buns. These were the size of large scones, slowly baked in the coal-fired oven. I made more biscuits as the range-riders hit the warming oven for seconds and thirds. It was a couple hours later before we got around to frying the fillets.

Immediately I was cast in the role of the cook. I had won my wings at the baking bin. I never had to brush or bran a horse thereafter.

On a cold night, after a day-long ride, I never liked the chores of hanging the saddle blankets up to dry, graining the stock, or those similar chores. I learned early that when the weather is warped, when the ice is talking back with your footsteps on it in sub-zero weather, camp cooking beats everything else.

I must confess I had had a little cooking in my younger years. My mother died suddenly with spinal meningitis when I was just starting high school. Those were Depression years, and I had to fill in while Dad worked nights and some days to feed the four kids.

Later in life, when I was "getting my year over with Uncle Sam's military," I wound up as a mess sergeant when Pearl Harbor fell hard upon us on December 7, 1941. Eventually I got a commission in the field artillery, but only after I had learned much about cooking — even army style. I could make a pink pancake, I knew where the mess sergeant steaks were on a side of beef. I could bake a cake, knead the biscuit dough — and open the corn flakes packet.

So perhaps I was justified in taking the lazy, warm-handed route — especially on a cold night in faraway Dutch John. I knew enough about horses to prefer the cooking. Also, having tasted the cooking of some others, I did not crave it. And this reason, more than any other, kept me kitchened.

The Day Gene Fullmer Sold His Horse

Gene Fullmer, former middleweight world boxing champion, was more than a fighter. He was an excellent horseman, deer hunter, and amateur fisherman.

One day we hunted deer east of Salt Lake City, in rather steep Mill Creek Canyon. Well, it's steep on the black-timber sides, and it's treacherous afoot if you hit the snow patches when they're iced up.

Gene liked to ride it rough. So did our partner that day, Dr. A. V. (Avaron) Osguthorpe, who knew that country like a book. His father had timbered it in the old pioneer days. And his grandfather had teamed out the heavy pine logs the generation before that. And from childhood Av had grown up with the wild game — for this was his land, in part, and he rode it pretty well every week.

But this day Av's knowledge went for naught. We found no deer as we ambled through the aspens, brushed the bitterroot and chaparral patches on the gentler slopes. We reasoned deer were in the black timber, shading up from the midday sun with their heavy winter fur on them. And the big bucks could hide in the pines better than anywhere else. So we took to the black timber on the icy north sides.

On the drive Av stayed in the canyon bottom; I took the

mid-mountain area; Gene topped out about fifty yards from the ridge, holding in the clear for anything that came over the top.

Gene was always in our view. Suddenly, while riding a snow patch, his horse slipped, lay on its side, and Gene and the mount came down the mountain. Gene stayed in the saddle as long as he could, hoping the horse would get a footing and right itself. Also, there was no alternative, as he explained later.

It was a bad fall on a steep slope. When I got to Gene he was standing with the reins in his hand, letting his horse rest on its side before urging it to its feet. There was still some mountain to slide on if the horse slipped again.

The horse finally got up, and Gene walked it to a spot under a pine tree where deer had bedded down. It was level enough there for both man and beast to rest a while. Gene's rifle was still in the saddle boot.

Gene examined the horse for scratches and bruises and found none. I had never seen Gene show so much concern about the looks of a horse — especially away from the grooming stall.

Then he told me the story.

This was one of his favorite horses in his stable of a dozen or more fine horses. Someone had offered him a fancy figure for the horse and Gene had accepted it. Delivery day was the next day. Gene had wanted one more ride on his favorite hunting horse.

I guess I was more concerned with Gene's well-being than the horse's at that moment. After all, he had a world championship to defend — and that purse would buy a lot of horses on anyone's market.

Nope, we never saw a buck that day. And a better day afield was never had by this hunter.

In fact, bagging a deer might have spoiled the day's sport.

We Couldn't Get the Kid's Rod . . .

No more fun in fishing than to see a kid catch fish.

Does something for the human heart.

There was one day when watching a kid catch fish got a little on our nerves. That was the time when two of us wanted to take the rod away from a successful young fisherman.

I was at Bullfrog Basin with Lewis Ellsworth, his son, Jim, and his grandson, Jimmy — and some others, including Lincoln White. We anchored our houseboat near the willows at the shallow end of Bullfrog inlet — where the almost unnoticeable Bullfrog Creek enters the large lake. It happened that the crappie, some about two pounds, had collected there, as fish will gather with their kind.

Using the houseboat as a base, we boated out in two fishing boats, each equipped with three or four anxious fishermen. For some reason we tried jigging for bass or crappie just a few rods from the houseboat and were soon catching fish. The best jig right then, in the semi-murky waters, was a small white crappie jig, headed by a pink floss. That jig caught fish when others failed.

We had only enough of those lures to go around — to the two Jimmies and me in my boat. The other fishermen had gone farther up the arm of the lake and we had lost communication with them.

Little Jimmy, for some inexplicable reason, had the hot rod and caught fish fast. At first his father took the fish off the hook for the five-year-old angler. This turned out quickly to be a one-Jimmy fishing trip — his father couldn't get a line into the water before young Jim had another crappie in the boat.

Jimmy was fishing close to the boat, and when his father could get to fishing big Jim and I made longer casts. Jigging close was for tiny tots. After all, casting was part of the sport, so we played it all the way. But whatever was beneath the boat was enough for our young angler. He filled a plastic bucket rather quickly, and Jim and I stood puzzled at his success.

Now and then we checked his hook to see if it varied in composition from ours. It didn't, as far as we could see. I had a card of those lures and had taken one for each of us — what was left of that card. The leader material was off the same spool of monofilament.

As a last resort we endeavored to get the rod from the lad to experiment as to its success. Did the kid have a touch we didn't have? Did he have mental perception with the fish? We had to know.

I have never known a lad who liked to fish as much as five-year-old Jimmy Ellsworth. And no one ever enjoyed catching fish, beating his dad and his dad's friend, like Jimmy did that day. He was like a tournament pro.

We thought we could slow him down by having him learn the hard process of taking crappie from his hook. But after he had been pricked by a dorsal spine once or twice we decided this was not a sporting approach. Then Jimmy-dad figured it might be well if we took little Jim to the houseboat and let him have a nap. After all, he had been fishing hard all day and the sun burn was showing on his young face.

That approach failed.

We studied the way the kid put the jig to the fish. No difference in his way and ours. Simple techniques.

We tried the hot hole near the boat. He caught fish and we didn't — except for a straggler now and then. The success ratio was something wider than five to one, and while it was fun to see the kid catch his fish the fact feathered us badly that there was some trick to his fishing. We were considered experts, big Jim and I. But this one stumped us.

We offered all kinds of enticements so Big Jim could get hold of Little Jim's rod — just to find out if it was the fisherman or the gear he was using.

My reputation, as an acute student of the pisces, was waning — in my mind as well as Big Jim's.

Napping for Jimmy was out. How about a run in the sand on the beach, or a swim in the lake (water was still cold that time of the spring)?

Time ran out on us, and as others returned to the houseboat we pulled anchor and drifted in. But we carefully marked that spot for the next day's doings.

Next morning, same routine! Even though we surreptitiously changed lures and leaders with the hot rod, the luck was all in Jimmy's favor.

We held a five-man discussion about crappie fishing and fishermen's fortunes while we were filleting a couple buckets of crappie. (There was no limit on the fish — and we liked crappie fillets as much as any fish we could catch in Utah waters.) We had five-times-five as many answers on why the kid could catch fish more than the rest of us and with the same fishing equipment.

Next day we cleaned many more and there was no solution to the Bullfrog riddle. In fact, while supper was simmering on the back burner, Jim and Lincoln boated to the marina, just before closing time, to buy a few more cards of white-pink jigs. That, we all figured, would give us a clue — help us have more success with our jig fishing.

After two days of bewilderment there was but one conclusion: kids and fish have a special relationship. Maybe kids can wish the fish on their hooks. At any rate, if it is a fish's fate to be caught on a human's hook, then let the kids have the honor of catching it.

P.S. Years have passed; Jimmy has grown to where he can lick salt off his pater's pate. He still has the fisherman's feel for fishing. He always fishes as if he were on the lucky side of Saint Peter's boat. Some fishermen have it!

The Case of the Big Pink Bear

Lennox Murdoch, who was my television boss during those first days on KSL, long before the co-axial cable came west across the Rocky Mountains, wanted to take his son, Bill, into the wilds somewhere — give the young man a real adventure in the big hills. I suggested the Wind River Mountains, east of Boulder, Wyoming. I had been there many times, and this, to me, was the place to see the grandeur of the mountains, have all the fishing you could take, and possibly see some interesting wildlife.

Lennox wanted that trip, and I gave him the name of Lloyd Kenney at the K-Spear Ranch (formerly the Pennock Trout Farm).

Lloyd would take Lennox and Bill into the Divide Lake area, and from there the two of them could hike to a dozen or more good fishing lakes. Kenney had a camp at Divide Lake. It was a good camp, except for the mess the bears made of it when Kenney or some of his campers were not around.

And that was just about every few days.

The camp was a torn-up mess when Kenney packed Lennox and Bill Murdoch into Divide Lake. It took some work to get things in order, and the broken cans of syrups and fats had to be discarded. But that was routine for Kenney's camp. For several years, Kenney had gone bear hunting during the season, but he had never been able to rid the Divide Lake region of his camp tramp.

Some years prior to the Murdoch trip, Enoch Eskelson and I, seeking a little adventure, went with Kenney into the Bounder Creek area to do a little fishing and sight-seeing. Lloyd was looking for sign of bear. He had some Kansas sportsmen booked for the bear hunt. He wanted to see if he could locate them a prize blackie. And the blackie he particularly wanted was the one he called the pink bear.

Pink?

According to Kenney, the bear was so old and wily that its hair had whitened with age to the degree that in the sunlight the bear looked pink. And this was the bear that was giving him all the distress at his dude camps. He knew that any time he was in the Divide Lake camp he was being watched by the old bruin and that as soon as he left the bear would come to the camp to get whatever was left.

So many times had Kenney vowed to kill the bruin that it had become an obsession with him. When in the area, he kept his saddle gun at ready. He looked for tracks, or fresh signs. But he had never set bait for the bear, nor made a big effort to get the animal. He just tolerated the critter; knew what to expect each time he left camp for a couple of days.

And in the many times we were in that area with Lloyd Kenney, we were always on the lookout for the bear. In fact, I preferred not to stay in the Divide Lake camp and usually chose to camp at Crescent Lake, four or five miles up the Middlefork Lake trail. So when Lennox asked about the camp and the area around and about, and what he should expect with the fishing, and if he should take a plunker gun for porcupine or ground hogs, I gave him all the data. And I stressed the fact that if he stayed at the Divide Lake camp he might keep an eye open for the pink bear. In this way he might alert Kenney as to the bruin's whereabouts.

I felt that my emphasis on the pink bear story put a tongue in Lennox' cheek. This sounded like a scare tactic — as if I were trying to make his simple horseback ride into the Wind Rivers something of an Alaskan adventure.

My cheek had a tongue in it, too. For as many times as I had looked for the bear, I had never seen it. Sometimes I wondered if there were such a critter. But I had been in some bear-eaten camps on the Middle Fork of the Salmon River, on the main Salmon (The River of No Return), and some other places.

Lennox and Bill Murdoch hadn't been back from their Wind River expedition but a few hours when I got a call. They had seen the pink bear, and Lennox told me the story as I listened in amazement.

When Kenney packed them into the Divide Lake camp, the camp itself was in pretty bad shape. Bear problems as usual. Rain was threatening, and Kenney, after the two Murdoch men had settled down, lined out down the trail to his ranch house — about ten miles away.

Lennox and Bill had an army hexagonal tent — like an abbreviated tepee. Just a two-man cover, with one slit opening in front, zippered. You got into it on your hands and knees. It was adequate, and when the rains came and the lightning flashed and the thunder cracked all around, Lennox and his son, who had just come home from a war stint in Korea, found themselves very comfortable. It could rain all it wanted.

Then the pink bear came on the scene and quickly gobbled up the few fish the two men had caught just before the rains came. Lennox had not told Bill what I had told him about the bear. Bill listened, and he could count each time the bear put one of the big paws down in the sloppy mud near the tent. The bear tore the kitchen tent, broke open cans, and scattered pans. It sounded like an army at work on a destruction assignment.

Bill admitted he shook from fright the entire time, but Lennox took it in stride. He had unzipped the tent about fifteen inches to let air in for the night. It was through this split the bear stuck his head — first came his nose, then, sniffing hard, he raised his head and tore open the tent to about three feet. One paw came into the opening and then part of the front shoulder. Bill recalls it was breaking day when their tent was "searched and sniffed."

Bill had a small automatic pistol, a .22 caliber. It was a luger-type which he intended to use on "porkies" or rodents of the mountain kind. Now he grabbed for the gun. Lennox restrained him without making a sound.

Lennox reached for a boot and then, as if he had been pricked by a hat pin between the hind pockets, he slapped the hiking boot into the face of the bear. At the same time he let out a terrible scream. The bear backed up and out and sauntered away as Bill fired several shots into the air and Lennox made more noise than he had ever made in his life.

The bear ambled to a spot 200 yards away, sat on its huge haunches, and looked back at the camp. The men dressed quickly. Soon the bear went off into the timber.

It would be another five days before Kenney would be back for them.

Like Lennox said, it might just have well been a bear fight every night thereafter. "We were jumpy from the time we went to bed until we awakened. And each night we were visited. We ceremoniously strung our catch of fish out each night — never too near the camp. Every night the bear would help himself to the catch, always take everything we hung out.

"We didn't want the fish in the tent, for obvious reasons. So we played the bear's game. What else could we do?

"By the time Lloyd Kenney came back for us, we had pretty good relations with the old pink bear. We never saw it again like we did that first night when he cased us pretty good. But we surely knew he was around — we could hear him snort as he wolfed down the fish."

Lennox said many times afterwards, as he recalled his trip to the Wind River Range with his son, Bill, "I thought you were blowing a big balloon with that pink bear story. But when you tell me a bear story again I will be the first to believe it." And even in repeating that story many times, Lennox Murdoch always turned a little pale when he did so. He never again wanted to have an opportunity to hit a big bear on the snoot from two feet away. Once was quite enough.

To my knowledge the pink bear still lives. Lloyd Kenney never got his dude hunters into the old bruin.

I'll Have to Ask Ben

Herman Franks of baseball fame had a fine black labrador retriever named Ben. Ben had been schooled properly, gone to dog college, knew more about duck hunting than the hunters who took him hunting.

Many times I hunted over Ben. One thing Ben did that irritated me was look at me in utter disgust each time I missed an easy shot. And I missed easy shots. So did Herman, for that matter, and Herman got the back of Ben's glove when he missed a bird.

Sometimes Herman would call me for a hunt; sometimes I would call him. He liked the way I cooked Italian sausage on the hibachi; so did Ben. This, if nothing else, made my company tolerable.

Herman had much respect for Ben, and he never asked Ben to go out in a cold marsh without Ben's okay.

One day I called Herman and suggested we go for the early shoot next day. There was a pause. "I'll have to check with Ben and call you later," Herman replied.

He called later. Ben didn't want to go.

I had so much respect for Ben as a retriever that I took both Herman and Ben at their words. Later I learned the whole truth: Herman was devoted to his pretty wife, Ami. And Herman never wanted to go hunting unless it was all right with Ami.

Now, Herman didn't want it to appear he was tied to Ami's apron. But he was, and he would always be first to admit it. He loved Ami and considered her wishes in every plan he made. Well, almost. I sat in the training camp dugouts with Herman when he was managing the San Francisco Giants and he did make some decisions those days in the Phoenix camps that Ami didn't have to approve — such as pinch hitters, etc.

Herman didn't want his friends to know about his total

devotion to his wife. After all, he was one of the toughest managers in organized baseball. No one would ever have guessed Herman was tied to an apron string.

So that's the story of Ben. Herman didn't ask Ben at all; he asked Ami. Ben and I talked it over one day while Herman was setting out decoys. Ben didn't make those decisions.

Between the two of us, Herman and me, we were possibly the world's worst duck hunters. We would set up a blind, light up the charcoals in the hibachi, and then wait for the coals to pink up. That not only kept our feet warm in the old barrel blinds but it provided us with a super grill. I had found the best Italian sausages in town — from Emil Smolka and his brothers at Modern Sausage — and we would spread out a sizzling sausage on that grill. I don't know how the ducks felt about it, but Herman and I had the marshes melting in sausage aromas. We had visitors, too, who had learned about our sausage shelf.

One opening day the ducks were flying all around us. Everyone was shooting. Herman and I sat back eating sausage sandwiches, watching the birds fly. Great show it was; and finally, when the dining was done, we got serious about shooting. But by then the flight had fatigued and we were left almost birdless.

Herman and I should have been given the conservation award of the year for our kindness to canvasbacks that season.

So Far and Yet So Close

I shall never forget one day in the Wind River Mountains and how we used the day's modern machinery to do what our forebears couldn't have done in weeks of time.

Herb Mulleneaux had asked me to speak at a morning Chamber of Commerce breakfast at pretty Pinedale — a little city which might well be dubbed the hub of the West's trouting world. I had many friends in Pinedale. And anyway, anyone who didn't enjoy a stop in Pinedale, with its surrounding mountain drop from the Wind River Range, wasn't very much alive.

It was a dress-up appearance, this breakfast assignment. And in Pinedale, in those days, dress up was with fishing vest, fly-ladened hat, waders (if you were in a rush), or any other garb you were going to be in the rest of the day. We had some fishing in mind — Herb had planned a day for us in one of his favorite sections of the Wind River Mountains. He had permitted me to bring along a fishing buddy, or two, or three.

The sky was just breaking dawn when George Folland lifted his four-passenger Cessna off the Salt Lake Airport and turned it, dead-beat, toward Pinedale. Along was Norm Bowen, a colleague at the *Deseret News,* and my son Michael.

In Pinedale I kept the speech short for two reasons: mine and theirs. I was going fishing, and Herb was seated closest to the exit so we could get to Fremont Lake in a hurry. Also, I didn't want to make a long speech on my fishing time. We both won, the breakfasters and the fishermen, with an abbreviated address that morning.

Joe Lunbeck of Pinedale had borrowed Earl Crandall's speedboat to take us to the inlet on the upside of Fremont Lake, about twelve fast miles from Monte Wight's dock and restaurant. I could have stayed the day, or a week, on Fremont Lake. It is a favorite spot for everyone, especially when the mighty mackinaw trout are testing a man's tackle. But Herb had other plans.

Quickly, as if time were running out on us, we took to a trail to Long Lake, steep as a rain pipe. At the top of this trail Herb had a canoe locked to a large tree. He opened the chain and quickly had the canoe on his head — like a long hat. He took it several hundred feet to the lake, slipped it in the water, and told two of us to get in. He paddled the length of the lake as his passengers trolled. They caught some nice cutthroats. Three of us shorelined the lake with our casting and fly rods and picked up a few feeders.

I could have stayed the rest of the day at that spot, but Herb soon had the canoe out of the water, rolled onto his shoulders with pads he had for carrying it, and was on his way to Wall Lake, not far up the trail.

Here he shuttled us to the inlet end of the lake, where we were in as wild a place as the Wind River Range can offer. I looked for fresh bear sign. Moose tracks were all around the lake. There were elk in the area and plenty of mule deer. If ever I felt like I was being watched by some unseen beings this was the day.

We had been out of Pinedale just a couple of hours and were in another world — a wild world. No paper plates, no boot tracks along the shoreline, no coke cans or bottle caps. This country was just as Charles Fremont left it back in 1831 when he left his mules at a base camp and set out afoot to scale the Wind River peaks — one of which bears his name.

The pools at the Wall Lake inlet were deep and clear. The fish were many, some large ones. They have had those waters so much to themselves these centuries past that the smallest movement stirred them. We felt like intruders. It was more sport to watch them than fish for them, although we did try our best flies on them, with little luck. Too spooky!

George kept watching the sun as it moved close to the western horizon. He had set a deadline to take off from the unlighted Pinedale airstrip. I almost hoped we would miss that deadline and remain at Wall Lake for another couple of sundowns.

George caught the biggest fish — about three pounds, wet weight.

Joe and Herb, incomparable hosts, sent us back with enough fish for supper, and breakfast, and lunch. These fish had never seen a hatchery pellet. They were of the same lineage that fed the Fremont party — no hybrids from the state hatcheries.

Herb watched the time as we started back. We did fish a few of the choice spots, and helped Herb with his canoe down the steep trails.

It seemed like only a few minutes from the top of Wall Lake to the Tim Holt dock at Fremont Lake where Earl Crandall kept his boat.

The afternoon winds were in George's favor as we waved goodbye to our hosts. We touched down on the Salt Lake strip just at dusk — right on time. As we tied George's plane down we reviewed the day. Could it have been possible? From Salt Lake City to the Wind River wilderness for a day of delightful fishing, and back again, all between dawn and dusk!

We promised to try it again. So far we have failed to keep that promise, but the memory of the day will be enough if we never get around to it.

Just Call Him Bow-Wow

His name was Wojciechowicz S. Wojtkiewicz. I don't know what the "S" stood for. I never dared ask him. But in kindness he said to call him "Bow-Wow."

He was an ardent fan of UCLA football team and a personal buddy of Coach Red Sanders. Also he was a friend of Don DeFore, the movie star who later made it big in television as Mister B in the Hazel program and in the Ozzie and Harriet productions.

When Don came hunting in Utah once, he brought Bow-Wow with him. "He's a phony," Don kiddingly said of his friend once when he introduced Bob-Wow to me and other hunting hosts.

He was far from that, as I came to know him as the years passed.

For instance, one night he and Don were bantering about their respective dislikes for each other, always kiddingly, when Bow-Wow said he wrote the Sheilah Graham Hollywood gossip column and if Don didn't mind his manners he, Bow-Wow, could cut him off all print.

That had to be the laugh of the season — Bow-Wow writing the Graham column — which was one of the best columns printed in those days.

"Not only that, I think I will marry her, and then you won't ever have a line of print," Bow-Wow challenged.

Don DeFore couldn't get over that boast — until he read in the columns that Wojciechowicz S. Woj — or Bow-Wow — was marrying Sheilah Graham. The marriage didn't last long. But some of us who thought the Beverly Hills man was tall in his talk had to eat crow pie.

Bow-Wow called a lot of shots. Jack Curtice had just left for Stanford, and the Utes were looking for a top-rate coach to take the Curtice place.

I was in Las Vegas on an assignment when I ran onto Bow-Wow. He said Ray Nagel, a brilliant young assistant to Red Sanders, would be the next Utah football coach. It was worth a rumor story, so I filed that night a scoop on this young assistant to Sanders who was near the top of the list, or atop it, for the Ute football coaching position.

Ray was chosen. Bow-Wow had hit it right on the head.

I saw Bow-Wow many times after that. Sometimes he came to Salt Lake to tend the Ray Nagel children while Ray and Shirley got in a little travel-proselyting time.

Bow-Wow's letters were gems, except that he never put on enough postage — just what he had available, like half-cent stamps. There were times when both the Post Office and I wished he wouldn't write.

Sometimes he would send nice cards and fake a lady's handwriting with such flattery as, "I think of you often," and sign it "Elizabeth Taylor." My wife knew Bow-Wow and the half-cent stamps, so I was never in trouble there.

Once we were stuck with Bow-Wow on a hunting trip we had planned with Don DeFore and Don's friends. All had brought guns but Bow-Wow. Knowing Bow-Wow as I did, I knew I would enjoy his company on the hunt.

He had gone to the supply room at UCLA and got an old football helmet and a football shirt, one worn by backfield players, with leather patches across the front — to hold the leather football against. He looked like something out of Red Grange days.

What to do with him?

We made a couple of drives and instructed Bow-Wow where to go and what to do. On one flat area in the aspen grove we always saw a few deer — two to four — and figured we could send Bow-Wow in the thickets to flush out the hiding buckskins. He picked up a gambol stick from an old quakie and started out. He started to sing and keep the beat with his stick, smacking it against the aspens.

We had posted ourselves strategically to cover the entire hill behind the flat area. Nothing could escape us.

Hand it to Bow-Wow, that was the most successful drive we ever launched through this familiar area. Thirteen deer came out, several of them bucks. Best drive of the hunt. Maybe it was the football helmet and playing shirt that did it.

Thereafter Bow-Wow had a standing invitation to be with us each deer hunt.

Maybe success went to his head. He never staged another drive for us.

A Diamond in the Rough

O. C. (Obert) Tanner is one of the best sports I ever knew. But I never knew him as a sportsman, an outdoor type, before we went fishing one day.

Lew and Jimmy Ellsworth, of insurance fame, had scheduled a float trip down the Green River from Flaming Gorge damsite to Little Hole, about eleven miles of cold, pure, fishable river.

All my life I had been running rivers, and sometimes I wondered if I was invited because I could row a boat with one hand and fish with the other. And that took care of one of the rowboats as far as manpower was concerned.

But then, I liked being with Lew and Jimmy and always made it a point to be on hand if they asked me to go with them. Like old Izaak Walton, the principled fisherman, said, "It is the company and not the charge that makes the feast." Also, I like rowing a boat. Sometimes it beats fishing. And fishing's hard to beat.

Obert and I took one boat and started out, rowing across the river to the first eddy so others could use the docking ramp. This gave me time to check Obert out with the fishing rod I had rigged up for him. We would start out with bait, garden worms, and he winced as he watched me thread the squirming worm on the hook.

I had sometimes been in Obert's company, spent some time at his beautiful home and yard in the region where, as a boy, I hunted rabbits in the fall of the year — long before Obert was anchored there. But those were social occasions. He and I had never fished together before. I didn't know if he was a fisherman; he didn't know if I was a boatman. So his concern this day about our respective talents might have been greater than mine.

I had read his books on philosophy and religion; he was a professor at the University of Utah in the philosophy area.

And that was a concern of mine that day — that we might have to fish the river philosophically. I preferred lures.

As is the way with fellow fishermen, you are cautious to be sure you in no way offend them — at least, at the start of a fishing day. We had to establish what one might call "ground rules."

He shrugged his shoulders with a grin of polite acceptance as I asked what fishing he preferred; as if to tell me he could do it all. So that decision was mine to make. Knowing the river, I decided to use bait and then anchor the craft by means of a heavy rock which I had acquired from the rampsite, anchor in some of the choice eddies. I had the river figured, so I thought each time I launched a boat on it. Most times I caught some fish — and some worth looking at twice.

I handed him his rod and clumsily he fussed with the Mitchell reel. I showed him how it worked, not knowing this was the first time he had ever handled one. He got the knack of that gadget quickly and lagged into the swift water, and the line almost skillfully eddied up where fish had to be. Instantly he had a bite and jerked the rod. A fat rainbow of about two pounds leapt into the air.

Lew and Jimmy floated by as Obert reeled in the two-pound fish. I netted it in due time and Obert was huffing and puffing as if he had just carried a hod of cement three stations up. The fish flopped all over the rubber raft as we admired it. Beautiful rainbow.

This early in the day we usually caught a few for Lew's lunch. He put them in foil, baked them with bacon. It was the highlight of the trip. We usually caught enough to eat and some to take home. Many we returned to the river.

What to do with his fish, however, was up to Obert. He was the captor. It was his fish. I suggested he might want to mount it, hang it on the office wall.

"Want to keep it?" I asked.

Still in shock over having a fight with a fish so soon after our launching the boat, Obert shook his head. I understood it to mean he wanted the fish returned. How gallant of this guy,

I thought at the time. He's a real sport to return a fish like that to the river. That's a display fish. He could put that in the show case of his Main Street jewelry shop and attract more customers than with some of those Royal Dalton dancers.

I gently took the hook from the fish's lips and returned the fish to the water. Obert watched intently and wordlessly. As the fish sank under the boat and then darted for the swift water, Obert kept his eye fastened to the fishing hole.

Fish gone, I freed the boat from the rock we were tied to and drifted in the eddy. Somehow I felt wrong about returning Obert's fish. He didn't respond to it as I thought he should. Finally I asked about it, reviewed the case.

"Obert, did you really want me to return that fish?"

He looked at me, knowing that we had misunderstood each other, and smiled.

"I thought you asked me if I wanted to kill it. And I thought I had better leave that up to you."

From that moment on Obert and I understood each other. We had our initiation. He had learned that if he is going to keep his best catches he had better stand up for his rights. From that moment he was a fisherman.

And try as we did that day, we could not duplicate Obert's rainbow trout.

Since that day we have had more than two pounds of laughs. Obert has told the story many times and so have I.

We agreed that the fish will grow bigger and some day we might all meet again — the fish, Obert, and I.

Another thing we agreed on was that this fishing story would also grow bigger with the passing of time — and it has!

But the fish, in the story, remains the same — a beautiful two pounds.

General John Charles Fremont

One night while a group of us was sitting around a Wind River Range campfire, talk turned to the history of that high mountain country. Who discovered it? Why were the peaks named Fremont? and Gannett? and Sacajawea? And why was the basin named for Titcomb? Who called it Island Lake? Who was the Wilson for which that mountain was named? How come a Mount Helen glacier?

Bill Worf was a Forest Service caretaker of that part of the world — to some of us the prettiest part of this planet. He had come across the diary of John Charles Fremont. He wanted to retrace the Fremont footsteps in that region, and he asked me to go with him.

My son, Scott, and I joined Bill in this venture. Ken Symes, Jerry Horton, Howard Shaw, Phil Johnson, Bob Sweedler and Bill Worf met us at Pinedale, Wyoming, our takeoff point.

We spent some time reviewing the diary, studying the maps, plotting Fremont's course and ours. We noted these salient first words:

"We left early, 15 of us on our best mules. . . . Soon we overlooked the valley . . . left our animals by a small creek . . . peaks were so close we chose to travel on foot.

"We became fatigued, slept the night on a flat rock, 100 feet from a little lake with an island near where a foaming torrent enters the lake. . . . I named it Island Lake.

"No breakfast. . . . We were away immediately. . . . Snow patches, falls, roaring water on all sides. . . . Pruess fell several hundred feet, just bruised. . . . I became ill and returned to Island Lake camp after sending Lajeunesse and four men back for mules and supplies. . . . Carson took instruments in the event he got to the summit . . . all returned that night without reaching the top.

"Rode mules as far as possible the next day to husband strength. . . . Put on light mocassins to dig toes into

snow. . . . Started up the main peak which I denominated
Snow Peak. . . . Here were three small deep lakes.

"We hiked deliberately, rested when tired . . . made way
rapidly near the top and sprang upon the sum-
mit. . . . Another step would have precipitated me into an im-
mense snow field 500 feet below . . . I stood on a narrow crest
three feet wide.

"It is presumed this is the highest peak in the Rocky
Mountains. . . . It was 2 o'clock when we left the summit. . . . Instruments showed the peak to be 13,750 feet above
the Gulf of California."

From this account Bill Worf figured Fremont and his party
made their base camp near Fremont Lake, maybe in the vi-
cinity of where Mary Faler's camp is — or in the timber near
the lake. They had to choose a place where their animals could
get feed from the flatlands.

When they took their best mules it is likely they went up
the trail now used by the Forest Service to get to Island Lake.
There is a shorter way, but it is no place for pack animals. I
have been both ways, and Bill and I agree that they likely took
the easier of the courses.

To get to Island Lake, Bill took us up the blazed Forest
Service route. Island Lake was not too far — something
around ten or twelve miles. Foot packers usually go this way
— it is rather a gentle climb to Island Lake. Few people know
of the steep pass through the cliffs around Wall and Long
lakes. Some of the Fremont party might have roamed this
virgin area in search of camp meat.

Island Lake is the takeoff point for Titcomb Basin, which
was cut by glaciers at the foot of the summit peaks of which
Fremont wrote.

We stopped at the sandy beach Fremont mentioned in
some parts of his diary — about fifty yards long and ideal for
taking a dip in Island Lake. Not far from the sandy beach is the
spot where the foaming torrent runs from Titcomb Basin lakes
into Island Lake. The water falls heavily over the rocks that
obstruct the main channel of the small stream.

Scott Miller looks over the Titcomb Basin pass at the foot of
Fremont Peak.

Scott and I stopped to fish this spot. It was such a promising trout hole we could not pass it by without making a cast or two. With a small black flatfish we caught half a dozen nice fish, mostly rainbows, and creeled them for supper that night. Scott also couldn't resist the foaming torrent Fremont wrote about. The fish in the stream were not as large as those in the lake.

We all stopped at the flat rock Fremont mentioned — where he came back and slept that night. He also wrote that it was on this flat rock he dropped his altitude instrument and broke the glass part of it. The rock was big enough to keep some of their supplies out of the damp tundra which was near the creek and the lake.

Then Fremont rode into Titcomb Basin. There have been times in my life when I have put my fly rod away and just ogled the scenery around me. Titcomb Basin was just such a place. It cast a spell over all of us. It is the most spectacular sight I have seen in that particular formation. I have seen the Alps, the Caucasus range east of the Black Sea, the Urals which divide Russia from Siberia, the Atlas in Morocco, the snow fields of Alaska around Mount McKinley, America's highest peak. They all have their scenic wonderments. But Titcomb Basin stands alone — or it did this day.

The snow was pinkish from the algae growth. The water was amethyst, tinted by glacial coloration. It is one of nature's dyes which remain mixed in the water, and in years of resting that color will never settle to the bottom. Every time one of our horses took a step, it walked upon some wild flowers. In select spots where any soil was seen, or if even a rock protruded above the snow, there was a flower in bloom. Some of them were brilliant in the red colors — like geraniums which hang from the windows in such quaint places as Bruges, Belgium.

The blue sky backdropped the peaks, offering the jagged pinnacles a mood of majesty. It is understandable that John Charles Fremont would conclude that his Snow Peak was the top of the Rocky Mountain world. It is far from that, yet as we sat in our saddles and turned our heads around like hoot owls to gather in all of the grandeur, it almost seemed that these must be the world's highest mountains.

I tried to compare them with Mount Blanc, which divides France, Italy and Switzerland. I liked those European Alps and have spent some time skiing them with Jack Simplot and Lowell Thomas. Still, to my mind the beauty of the Wind Rivers surpasses all others.

Scott too passed up the fishing. And I never thought I would see the day when this would happen. As he said, "It just seems the fish belong in these waters, and it seems wrong to remove them from this beautiful basin. That would be like stealing the stars from the heavens."

And so it would.

Chuck Keefer's World Record Brown Trout

Not in every generation is there a change in the world record fishing books. The German brown trout record, for instance, has stood since 1866. It was caught by Mr. W. Muir in Loch Awe, Scotland. The fish weighed thirty-nine pounds, eight ounces.

Everyone in the sports fishing world accepted that listing because *Field and Stream* magazine forever published it as official. So when Chuck Keefer of Dutch John went out one January morning, in a place where the ice was not forming on the Flaming Gorge Reservoir, and boated his thirty-one-pound, twelve-ounce brown trout, he could only claim a state record.

Let's start at the beginning of the Chuck Keefer story. Here is a piece I wrote for the Dardevle Annual Fishing Book at the request of Dardevle's president, Ed Eppinger:

In the middle of any January, Dutch John, Utah, near Flaming Gorge Reservoir, is no place to be shirt-sleeving it! But January 25, 1975, the sun broke through for several days and fishermen filed out from their midwinter firesides to look upon the lake and its surrounding landscape.

One of these was Chuck Keefer, who worked daily at the damsite and who spent whatever time he could spare spanking the lake's waters for assorted trout.

At Dutch John, as remote an outpost as you can find, what better way to spend time than at the lake — which is what the area has most to offer its residents.

Chuck and his wife, Carlene, with Darwin Rutledge, a friend, and Darwin's twelve-year-old daughter, Carol, launched their boat and motored uplake. This was the first January in the reservoir's history that ice had not covered the lake in the narrow canyons. This fact, more than any, drew the Keefers' attention.

Four or five miles from the marina they let out trolling lines, hoping for mackinaw trout. But this was not the day for macks. No bites! Near the top or on the bottom! With a couple of lines out, and trying all lures, the Keefers and Rutledges gave up.

Going back, Chuck pulled near the rocky shoreline where cedar trees and pines come to the lake's edge. Chuck always liked the shoreline in this spot. Also he had kept in mind the large brown trout his neighbor, Verl Hanchett, had caught several months before. It was a new Utah State record at twenty-nine pounds, eight ounces. That's a big fish.

Also there had been some fifteen and twenty-pound trout boated and, as is the way with fishermen, some lunkers, estimated to be records, had broken tackle and got away. Knowing this, Chuck had to make a few casts while they were sopping up that midwinter sun. From his small and rather rusted lure box, he took a red and white Dardevle spoon, one that was well knocked about. On ten-pound-test line, with a spinning reel and a rather willowy rod, Chuck shot the spoon toward the shoreline and then sat back to let it sink. At about thirty feet he started to retrieve it.

"Thought at first I had hit a ledge and locked up," Chuck said. "But it moved and I knew I had a fish, and a big one. They had been taking a lot of big fish of the fifteen-pound range, and I thought it was one of these. So I took pains to adjust the drag on the line, to be sure I kept him away from the shoreline.

"By then everyone wanted to take a look, and we all watched as the big fish started to yield to the pressure of the ten-pound-test line. You always worry about the knot in your line — whether it would cut itself or 'fracture' with the pressure.

"It might have been ten minutes before I saw the fish and — magnified in the water — I thought I had a whale. The fish yielded easier than I thought it would, and later, when cleaning it, I learned why. It had several fish in its stomach, one of which was a fifteen-inch rainbow trout. Evidently it was on a gluttonous feed right then, and with a bellyful it was not in a mood to tow us up and down the lake.

"We realized we had a big one when we got it into the net and tried to lift it in the boat. But it didn't look any larger than the brown trout Hanchett had caught."

Hanchett, a state conservation officer, was at the marina dock when Keefer came in. "He shook his head and said we should get it weighed right away. He figured it was bigger than his, and the fact that he had caught a state record brown trout made everyone aware of the size of fish the lake was producing.

"We rushed to the post office, which didn't open until mail came late in the afternoon. We waited for most of an hour and then weighed it on the mail scales — which are about as accurate as scales come. I had beat Hanchett — it weighed thirty-one pounds, twelve ounces. Hanchett got out the record book, and it appeared we had beaten the American record. At that point we double-checked all weights and measurements to be sure of accuracy. They checked out. I had enough witnesses to make proper affidavits, and suddenly I found me and my fish getting involved in record keeping. I never had to worry about all that stuff before. I just caught the fish, cleaned them and ate them.

"With a possible record, what then? We had the necessary data on the fish, substantiated properly. Next step, as Carlene suggested, was to keep the fish fresh for mounting. In the freezer it went."

Several weeks later Chuck and Carlene accompanied me on the lake and I asked him to repeat the technique which he used in taking an American record brown trout.

"It's easy," Chuck chuckled. "Take me close to the shoreline.

"Now you rig up this rod, and pull a bit at the line to test its strength. Then you open your lure box and pick out the lure you've caught the most fish on, which is this small, two-inch red and white spoon." (He was a Dardevle man from way back and had nothing but Dardevles in his box — and mostly red and white ones.)

"You tie it on like that, and cast it ten feet from the shoreline and let it sink."

He made sure I was watching — and I was.

"When you think it's about thirty feet deep you start your retrieve, about like this." He cranked the reel slowly.

"And then you set the hook when you feel the fish strike."

He went through the motions of hooking the fish. But this time there was no bite.

"Sometimes you hit them and sometimes you don't. And sometimes, if you're a very lucky fellow, you hook into the largest brown trout ever caught by hook and line in America.

"Isn't that easy?"

"And some day someone is going to do just like I did and find this fish's grandpa. And there will go my record!"

Not long after Chuck had caught his record trout, the Utah Division of Wildlife, while making scientific studies of fish growth in the lake, gill-netted a forty-four-pound brown trout in Lynnwood Bay near the Lucerne Marina, midway up the lake. They weighed it on their unofficial boat scales and released it in good condition.

The fisherman who boats that monster and any others like it will have a new world record. Perhaps it will be the present holder of the North American brown trout record. Chuck Keefer. After all, he has the technique, and the right lures to do it.

Follo Dardevle quote:

And so the Keefer story remained until a year later, when some interesting news broke in Charles Keefer's favor. Chuck Keefer received a letter from Larry Ramsell, secretary to the United States Fresh Water Fishing Hall of Fame, world's records keeper. It read:

"Dear Chuck: I am sending you a copy of the news release that went out this week (dated March 24, 1976). I am also enclosing part of the letter from the British Record Fish Committee, which maintains the record books in Great Britain where the 39-8 fish was taken in Scotland.

"I thought you should know the whole story."

The letter from Great Britain was signed by P. H. Tombleson, secretary of the British Record Fish Committee. It was addressed to Larry Ramsell. It was dated Jan. 19, 1976, and it read:

"You mention two salmonids which were listed presumably from the *Field and Stream* list.

"The brown trout of 39 pounds, 8 ounces, which was caught in Loch Awe in 1866 by Mr. W. Muir, was foul-hooked and ineligible. The *Field and Stream* list must be out of date."

That brought great joy to United States freshwater trouters. Chuck Keefer had an official world record for brown trout caught on rod and reel.

Actually Mr. Muir would not have had a record for a foul-hooked brownie.

About the time the Keefer finny was pronounced an official world champion, the researchers for the Utah Division of Wildlife, while seining in the flat waters near Manila marina, gill-netted a forty-four pound trout. They weighed all fish they netted, tagged them and returned them to the lake.

At first the big fish was kept a secret. But someone soon leaked the word out to this writer and I told the world about it. Why not?

We know there is a larger fish than the Keefer keeper down in those depths. Every fisherman has dreamed he would be the one to get it to gaff and to stand with the pictures being taken, heralded as the holder of the world record. Until that dream comes true that honor belongs, at least for a while, to Chuck Keefer of Dutch John, Utah. And a worthy world record holder he is!

Note: *The world record held by Chuck Keefer was subsequently broken.*

From Tennis to Trout

Tony Trabert was the world's best tennis player. He had just won the United States Open Championship. He had won the Davis Cup Singles — and most every tournament in which he played.

He fell in love with a Utah girl of note, Miss Shauna Wood. And Shauna had won every beauty contest she entered. I knew about Shauna because I was on many of the panels which judged the beautiful ladies in those days. She was a constant winner and was chosen as the Miss Utah for the Miss World contest in the early 1950s.

After Tony and Shauna were married, Tony became interested in Utah's recreation facilities, and one day he asked me to take him fishing.

Scofield Reservoir right then was noted for its evening fly fishing, so Tony and I headed that way one afternoon. I had been to the lake earlier and had good results. Shauna gave Tony some time off for the fishing trip provided he returned with some trout. Shauna liked trout. Her father, Brick, might have caught a few in his day for his family table. I promised Shauna that we would return with some fish.

Here is the report of that trip as I penned it for the *Deseret News*, dated August 7, 1954:

Trabert Wins His Fishing Set, 5-3;
Scofield Fly Fishing Still Tops.

The wind was high at Fred Warner's boat camp on Scofield Reservoir's west shoreline. Fred said we would not do any good today. His partner, Ed Miller, agreed with that forecast.

"Our no. 9 boat came in a few minutes ago and they didn't have a bite. Been fishing all morning. It rained all night and the blow has been bad all day," Fred said.

We had traveled quite a ways to get there and were fevered about a little fishing. I just couldn't take Fred's advice that we give it up.

A young athlete named Tony Trabert had set one day aside to go fishing in Utah during his rest from tennis (he's U.S. National champion — that's the best). I told him the fishing was great at Scofield and we could have a good day of it — if the weather didn't kill us. Right then we were dying fast.

Fred Warner cocked his weather-beaten bonnet as he set us adrift in one of his boats a few minutes later. There were just the two of us, so we were floating light.

"Maybe this is not your kind of weather," Tony said, as if to chip in a little cheer right then. "But this is great. Look at those mountains and those clouds. We have enough to eat, a thermos of lemonade and a raincoat. What more is there?"

"Just a good catch of fish," I answered, as I started the little motor which I had won in a national hunting and fishing contest the month after I had come home from five years in World War II.

I was concerned about our fate. Tony had been so excited about getting out in the Utah wilds for a day, and I had told him how good the fishing was and would be, that I felt very responsible for the man's time and that it be used enjoyably. That meant one thing: catching fish.

We had stopped in Provo City to buy worms in the event we needed to use bait while waiting for the sundown fly fishing.

A young man had come home from school to get some of the books he left and was there to help us. I introduced him to Tony Trabert, the world's greatest tennis player, and he ran off to school to tell his playmates, and maybe some of his teachers, about his few minutes with Tony Trabert.

Tony and I chuckled about the kid's enthusiasm. The lad wanted to donate all the worms we needed to the cause of tennis. But we wouldn't let that happen. Tony gave him a silver dollar and told him to buy his mother something with it. (Hope he didn't do that — and saved the silver dollar so he could now buy his mother so much more with it.)

It was 2:30 P.M. when we got to the lake that afternoon. We headed toward Jap Point to find shelter from the wind. That's where we had caught them a week ago. We anchored and baited and cast a few lures. No luck!

I caught one perch on bait after moving to four different spots.

We had to find the fish, so we rigged up for trolling and headed for the east shore. Still no action.

There was one boat anchored on the downwind side of the island. We soon joined it.

As we cruised into the small cove the lady in the other boat landed a nice trout. We thought we had found the fish.

We did find two trout and several perch. Tony, skunked to this hour, never gave up. He finally got the knack of feeling his line, keeping it taut in that high wind, and setting the hook at the neatest nibble.

I had the tennis champ thirty-love on trout when he finally hooked into a charged-up rainbow.

Tony's an amateur at tennis by request of the Lawn Tennis Association and the Amateur Athletic Union. But he's a pro when it comes to contending against an aroused rainbow trout. Give him a week at this action and he would beat all of us, backhand, forehand, volley, with any stroke.

Tony had an injured right hand, but when he gave that fish the backhand stroke I thought he would turn the trout inside out.

Tony broke a wide smile as we lifted a nice rainbow into the boat. Three trout — we at least had breakfast for Tony.

We watched the sun close the western gap. We knew from experience at Scofield that when the shade of the western horizon fell over the lake the trout would come to the top to feed on the midge hatch.

One fly fisherman nearby was ahead of the sunset with a nice rainbow, and this seemed to wake up the whole west side. We knew then it was time to get the fly rods out for the evening — put everything else away.

About twenty cars were parked along the west shoreline. Other fishermen knew when to be at Scofield, and just before the sun set it seemed the whole mountain came alive as fishermen waded into the lake from the mountainside road.

Unlike the winds earlier in the day, there was not a ripple of any kind on the lake — only the one created by the fishermen as they waded far enough into the lake to clear space for their backcasts. Tony and I stayed in the boat, fishing toward the shoreline. We figured we had an advantage.

So calm was the evening that no one caught fish. No riffles on the water. Dead!

Sometimes in the past I had made my own riffle, and so in desperation I suggested to Tony that we troll our flies. This, I reasoned, would give action to the lake's surface, and we needed that right then.

As soon as Tony got his line out he had a nice tail-walking rainbow on. We made one small loop, several hundred yards from the shoreline so we would not spoil the fly fishing for others who had waded into the lake from the shore. We caught two trout on that loop. I lost my leader and flies to a lunker that was too much for me.

By the time it got deep dusk and well into the night we had a nice catch of trout — eight of them over a pound in size.

His wife Shauna had let him go fishing only under the condition he would bring back some fish. It had looked for a while like we would have to stop at a fish market en route home.

Several times Tony laid out the fish just to look upon them, like he would admire a fine piece of art.

Just at quitting time the rains came and we hurried in. We found our way only because Fred had kept the light burning at the boat ramp.

Tony had won another match. The score with the big fish that day was five sets to three, advantage Trabert!

The Utah Aggie Deer Hunt

Back in the days when Tony Knap and Ev Faunce coached football at Utah State University, the Aggies had an annual deer hunt. It was a traditional event.

It started this way.

Bob Wilson, a fine end for USU, talked his father-in law, Alva Dearden, sometime mayor of Henefer, into a deer hunt on the Dearden property in the Chalk Creek area for a few of Bob's football friends. From a simple beginning this would turn into quite an outing, with even the coaches joining in the hunt for the big buck.

In those days there were no full-furnished training tables for the athletes. They got an occasional meal. NCAA allowed them fifteen dollars spending money provided they worked for it, and fifteen dollars didn't buy many beans or much bread. A deer in the cooler was the handsomest handout some of those athletes could have. It was a matter of having something to eat on those cold winter days at the boarding house. It was arranged that someone in Cache County would have the buckskins butchered, and someone else would keep them in a cooler. But while the meat was a considerable item, so was the sport of having a hunt in some of the world's best deer country.

One of the side benefits for the coaches was the recruiting advantage. The Utah Aggie deer hunt became famous, and some athletes signed up for Utah State football on the basis of the hunt. Some even bought deer rifles and included the guns in their luggage when they reported for school. And the talk about the deer hunt went around the country. The coaches used it in convincing a big tackle that part of his adventure at Logan's USU would be to hunt the big mule deer on the Cache National Forest. Many athletes over the years confessed this was the "goodie" which tipped the scales in USU's favor.

Coaches planned the hunt when Utah State had a home

game. As soon as the players could change from their game pads to their sweat shirts and Levi's they were headed for the hills. Sometimes they made it to Henefer in time to take one ride around the rim to look for the sunset browsers on the high points. But then they had all day Saturday, and some skipped Monday classes to hunt part of the next day.

Most everyone got a buck. Alva Dearden, Rulon Francis, Bob Wilson and I saw to that. We could find plenty of hunting time during the week, so we let the footballers have the harvest. Many times we had deer piled on top of the cars, in the trunks, and even stuffed in the back seats. So loaded were some of the cars or trucks that the body of the cars were solid against the axles. No springs could take that overload.

I remember one drive we made. We saved the big canyon until the afternoon, when all fourteen of us could make a drive. Seldom did we have this many people on a single sortie. And how often we wished we had more hunters to handle the one big canyon! We needed numbers of hunters to keep the deer contained.

Alva and Bob organized the drive: Some of us would be on the rims; others would stay in the bottom; others would brush part of the way up the hills — to push the deer toward those who were posted in the right places when the bucks went out of the canyon. The ridge runners would leave first and get positioned on designated points. They would be able to see in front of them and back of them — watch the whole show once it started. The side-hillers and the bottom boys left together, each being instructed where possible to watch the faces of the mountain across the canyon from them.

As expected, the first shot stirred up the herd. Deer went everywhere. You could hear the hunters yell to each other about their success or failure. Each told the others if a deer broke brush ahead of them. It was like the football defense alerting each lineman as to where the ball runner was hitting the hole in the line.

There was a lot of chatter, and that helped move the mulies. And as a result of the commotion there was plenty of shooting. For a while it sounded like the artillery barrage in the North African campaign, when the Yanks were chasing the Germans' Afrika Korps.

In due time we gathered at the rendezvous point at the bottom of the canyon. Each hunter was to bring out his own deer. Some came wearing their three-point bucks around their necks like milady would wear a fox cape. Why not? After all, these were well-conditioned, 250-pound tackles.

The fourteen of us killed seven bucks in that drive. That was enough to keep these Aggies in preferred protein for the winter. We staged other drives and added a few more mulies.

Coach Faunce kept a good count of his men. He didn't want to leave one on the hill — and miss football practice. When just about everyone was gathered, resting up a bit before the next drive, hanging their deer in nearby trees to cool out, Coach Faunce had a roll call.

"They're all here," Evvy said. "Gee, then I must have shot a deer."

Coming from the coach, the pun was not as funny as puns should be. There was concern, though, about the safety of all the hunters; this was the first deer hunt for many of them. But then, they had studied the rules of the range and were prepared to be cautious and aware of another's presence in the hunting area.

That got to be the joke for many years thereafter — "If they are all here, then I've shot a deer!"

On another Utah Aggie deer hunt we went into Coal Hollow early in the morning, hoping to spot a browser on one of the canyon sides or on the points. That's called road running, and at sunrise and sunset it's the best way to cover the most deer territory.

Some rode in the cab of the truck. Others rode in the truck bed; all ogled the landscape for that white patch of the mulie known as its behind.

About 150 yards into Coal Hollow we saw a couple of bucks standing on a point. They looked up from their browsing to watch us. We tapped the cab of the truck and the driver stopped.

Len Rohde, all-conference lineman and later on outstanding professional player, had spotted the animals. He got out of the truck and paused, looking at Hy Hunsaker, athletic director.

"Just look at this first one," Len said to Hy. Hy was looking.

"What you going to do about it?" Hy asked Len.

Bam! The buck slunk into the hill.

Len just stood there, almost in shock.

"Go get it!" Hy told Rohde.

And he went, busting brush up the steep incline like he would rip into an opposing line in a title game. One of the other gridders set aside his gun and took off with Rohde. The other deer had hid in the brush, and as the two men approached the scene the smaller deer bounced into another thicket and no one got a shot at it.

We watched as the two came up short of the carcass by about eight yards. We pointed the spot to them and they quickly found their buck. They stood around as if to admire their prey, when all of a sudden Len got downhill from the buck and started to sling it over his shoulders. He got an assist, and the two men made a beeline for the truck — like Rohde would carry an opposing guard on his shoulders until the whistle to stop had been blown. Len laid the deer as gently on the ground as he would an injured teammate.

We guessed he had never dressed a deer, so we all gave a hand and we had the innards out and the hide off in just a few minutes — and the deer tagged and hanging in a shaded area to cool while we continued to hunt.

This was the day for the younger hunters to get their meat, to fill their winter larders.

There was one special place where we could make a drive with a half-dozen men, and we saved this spot for our first drive that day. It was a flat area with an open sidehill as a backdrop. The flatland was heavily covered with aspens, and it would take some good drivers to beat out the bucks. We had some good brushers. I considered myself one of the best —

mostly because for many years I had worked this area, and with great success.

I chose to drive the middle of the forest. Taking a large stick, a dead branch from an aspen, I beat a tattoo upon the trees as I walked through the area. All the hunters were posted at key places — we were especially interested in the sidehill where the deer had to go. We had them "fenced in" on the downside of the flatland.

There was no shooting, which surprised me as I neared the end of the drive. There was one small pocket of brush left on this drive, and I thought it best to go right through to the steep face of the hill. Suddenly, as if I had been ambushed, a large buck, a majestic four-pointer, broke out of the thicket. He was cornered and I was his obstacle right then. He had to come my way, and I hit the ground as he jumped over me. All I could see was his underside. There was no time to fire a gun, even from the hip. You can't fire from the hip when you're flat on your belly in the brush.

I got a good look at the animal's eyes. He was scared.

It happened that Bus Williams, one of the Aggie coaches who later became athletic director, was on the point where the first clearing was. Bus would have at least two hundred yards of open space to do what he could about the fleet buck. Bus missed the first shot; he didn't miss the second.

That was the only buck we brushed out of this choice area. But it's a buckskin this hunter will never forget. How often a hunter carries his gun at ready hoping for hand-to-horn combat — a case just like this one! This time I had my chance at that once-in-a-lifetime adventure with a monarch buck, the kind of shot you dream about.

When it came right down to it, this brave man wound up on his belly in the brush.

I Hope Those Buzzards Drown

In the middle of the 1950s the Idaho Coaches Association, a group of high school mentors, staged one of the country's best sports clinics at Sun Valley, Idaho. It was an annual event.

Jerry Dillinger, of Jerome, who headed up the clinics most of those years, always asked me to attend their big football and basketball show, and I seldom missed a chance to be there. It was opportunity to mingle with the prep coaches and also some of the college greats at the time.

I found it convenient to skip some of the classes in the interest of writing time for my daily column with the *Deseret News*. This also gave me a little recreation time, and the best time I could spend in self-happiness was to be on the Wood River down by the Red Motel or on the Silver Creek near Bellevue. At Ketchum one night I checked in with the fishermen I knew, and they all leaned toward fishing Silver Creek. It was red hot for fly fishing right now.

My wife, who is tolerant about my fishing as a wife should be, waited patiently while I checked out the best fishing spots. Also I wanted to have the right fly patterns if I went to Silver Creek.

I was told that the grasshopper crop was heavy and the fish were taking hoppers from the overhang grasses. I bought some hopper patterns, just in case. I was a veteran hopper fisherman, however, and my dear old daddy had taught me well in using the natural baits. He would take a small bare hook, or a fly hook that was sparse in its hackle or feathers, and then with a small loop of sewing thread he would wrap the hopper's thorax to the hook's shaft. This would let the hopper have all its legs and squirms — just as the fish found them when they hopped upon the river's surface.

I had my usual assortment of flies, patterns I thought would work for trout any time and on any water.

En route to the river east of Bellevue I stopped by a parked truck to ask its passengers about closed waters and where I might enter the river without trespassing upon anyone's premises. The two men and their wives, all four in the seat of the truck, were on the way to the river. They had their boat for the river float riding a small trailer, and the truck loaded with oars and floating gear.

As I came broadside to them, in the early hours of the day, I noticed the men were having a nip of old grog. They were giddy, and maybe this was in my favor, for they took all the time I needed to tell me all about the river. I would have rowed the boat for them if they had asked me but they didn't. They told me to go to the railroad trestle and park there and fish the stream from that point. This was the point where they intended to end their float — they would be drifting through private land most of seven miles.

I did as they told me and found the fishing superb. As I had been told, the fish were after the grasshoppers which sometimes made the wrong jump into the river. Also there was a hatch of small flies on the water, and the fish were hard against the grassy banks nipping all the gnats and hoppers that came into the river from the shoreline. It was a heavy feed — the kind a fly fisherman likes to look upon as he enters a fishing place.

I tied up an Adams pattern, and with long casts let it fall upon the grass across the river. Then with small jerks I freed it from the grass and it fell upright upon the water.

Every good cast brought a strike, I was using small hooks, and losing a good share of the fish that hit my fly — just nipped them in the lips. Later, with some large-hook hopper patterns, I caught a better percentage of the fish that struck my flies. In an hour I had a full quota of nice rainbows — some to three pounds. I wanted to take a limit of fish back to Sun Valley for a special trout dinner for Jerry Dillinger's special guests. There's something extra special about a trout dinner if the trout have just been caught.

As I walked through the grassy fields to where I had

parked the car, I noticed that the two women I had talked to earlier in the day were there waiting for their boating husbands to come down the river. The ladies had set their rods at one of the inactive spots along the river, where nary a trout would be. And they were still nipping at the bottle.

I stopped to thank them for their advice. I had been successful on what information they had offered me. They asked about my luck. I displayed my catch. Seldom have I seen a better spread of red rainbows. This was something to behold. The sun was still on the morning side of the day, and the trout glistened in the green grass I had bedded them with in my basket.

The ladies took a sobering look at the fish. One confessed, I thought glibly, "I would like to have a mess of fish like that when our husbands come — to show those two drunks we can catch fish, too. This driving truck, and tending camp for those men is for the birds — the ravens. I've hoped all morning that their boat would tip over."

We chatted a bit as the sun rose higher in the clear blue sky. I could see the fish grabbing those flies and grasshoppers at every bend of the river — as far as I could see the river.

"Would you like these fish?" I offered.

They would like them, and already they were planning the fish stories they were going to tell those "buzzards" when they saw them again.

That was the prettiest catch of fish I ever gave away. I had planned to display them to the coaches at the clinic before I had the chef at the Inn fry them for the guest coaches.

I had no choice but to turn around and go fishing again. One of the ladies walked along with me as we fished the next bend. But now the fish just wouldn't pay any attention to my flies. I put those tiny Adams flies on the top as daintily as they could be placed — but no results.

With my spinning rod, which I had brought along, I tried a lure — a rather large spoon. Casting upstream, I brought the lure quickly down current in the moss lanes, and most every cast I had a strike. I soon had four or five nice rainbows for the lady who stood watching me. We were amazed at how the lure worked and with what success.

Again she was plotting in her active mind how she would get herself a spinning outfit, practice in her back yard, and next time be glad to drive the trailer to the trestle while the men boated leisurely down the creek those ten miles or so. She was a good student and soon the other lady came to watch. I was a good teacher and showed them exactly how it was done. We went to several bends in the river, and each time I caught fish. To prove a point, I took the largest lure I had, about a five-inch blade, and tried it. It produced better than the rest.

Soon I had my third limit of fish — one each for the two ladies and one for the coaches at the Sun Valley clinic. I cleaned the fish and laid them in a grassy nest, as fine a display as one would want to look upon.

The women made one deal with me. They would tell their husbands they caught the fish. And if I saw the two men upriver and had a chance to speak to them, would I play the game — tell the men that their wives had limited up and were waiting for them to come so they could go home?

I never saw the men. I have often wondered what stories were told them that day.

The lady had changed her mind about "drowning those buzzards." Now she wanted them to see her fish. If they drowned, she would have no one to tell her story to.

Hunter From Hollywood

Utah celebrated its centennial year in 1947. It had been one hundred years since Brigham Young led the pioneers to the Salt Lake Valley. Part of that centennial celebration was the annual governors' convention. The most noteworthy governor on the political scene at that time was Thomas Dewey, then a "shoo-in" for the office of President of the United States. But Thomas Dewey never got shooed in. A haberdasher from Independence, Missouri, beat him out in the November election.

Another fringe benefit of the Centennial was the premiere of the movie *Ramrod*.

This movie, a messy western, was directed by Andre De-Toth, who had never seen either Indian or cowboy, or range rifle. It was tabbed with a Salt Lake City opening, and got a lot of play because of the Centennial. Many top-rate actors and actresses were involved in it. One was Don DeFore, who had come up to stardom with the Hal Roach productions.

Don was a likeable sort, and he was invited by Governor Herbert B. Maw, another likeable sort, to return to Utah at his pleasure for a deer hunt.

Governor Maw was not in the state when, that fall, Don decided to come up for a hunt. He had a break in his Hollywood castings. The governor's office turned Don and his hunting party over to this author. It was not often our lot or pleasure to host Hollywood dudes, but our years of hunting and fishing with Don DeFore, his brother, Verne, and a friend named Jack Rau, turned out to be pleasant experiences.

Don hardly knew what he wanted to hunt when he got to Utah. He had checked out an old hammer-type Winchester shotgun from the studio supply shop. What an antique that was, as I learned later when I checked the head space and breech for dangers!

I had drawn a permit to hunt elk, and nonresidents could

not hunt elk in Utah. Elk, then, was out of the question. The deer hunt was not on. So we were stuck with ducks — and duck hunting is fun to be stuck with.

Merrill Hand of Draper and Dooley Nelson of the Farmington Bay Bird Refuge gave us a hand. Lynn Hansen, a sporting goods dealer at the time, also helped. In Dooley's airboat we took the hunters onto the mud flats bordering the Great Salt Lake. We went way out into the pintail flight. The pintail ducks come into our west from Canada on their way south — by the millions. Not many canvasback, mallard or even spoonbill come, mostly "pins."

On the mud flats, building the blinds is a problem. We had taken a hundred or so metal silhouette decoys to stick up in the mud, but Dooley and Merrill had some additional ideas. While some of us shoveled the pits, these two men worked on setting up mud decoys — just turning over mud, letting it stick up about five inches above the water level.

Once we got the blinds built and the decoys in place, Dooley took the airboat several hundred yards from the hunting area and we settled down for a good shoot. And we got it. The limit was four birds per hunter — which, to some, hardly made it worth the effort of going hunting, especially with what we did in the mud flats that day.

Don and I had one of the blinds. We were far enough from the others to have our own shooting.

Earlier in the day I had checked Don's shotgun. It was a risky gun. It had been used on the movie set for years — an oldie. Its head-spacing was questionable. It rattled when you held it still. It was a hunk of junk to any duck hunter.

Diplomatically I traded him guns. I wanted him to try my new five-shot Browning automatic, and in a few minutes I schooled him well in its use. It was legally plugged to the three-shell limit.

Don had never hunted moving ducks, or sitting ones. All that movie-set shooting was fakery, and Don admitted it as a preface to our shoot. He apologized early for the birds he was about to miss.

And he missed some.

The flight was good, and I told Don to get his four and then I would get mine. After he missed some first birds, I decided I would have to back him up. With one shell at a time I loaded his old Winchester firing stick. When he missed a target I would get in one shot. I hit a few birds. He had not done enough shooting to know whether he hit the bird or not. Nor was I sure about it.

I flattered him each time a fowl fell. Sportingly he would get out of the blind and chase the ailing or dead duck through the thick mud. I liked that part of the hunt. I had my own retriever, and a happy retriever, at that.

Compared to my dramatics that day, Don DeFore was a ham amateur. Sometimes I must have overacted the part. "What a beautiful shot that was," I would exclaim each time I shot at a bird he had missed. "You're getting the knack of it now," I would add. He might have hit all the birds that day, or most of them.

But he chased all of them. Each time a duck was downed Don would volunteer to chase it down. It flattered me that my dramatics were that good. I was getting away with more than I deserved. I figured I killed all eight birds — or seven at least. Don figured he got his limit and mine. We had killed, in our way of thinking, sixteen birds, and yet only had a legal limit of eight. Beat that for a busy day!

Next day was the elk hunt, and in the annual drawing Lynn Hansen and I had drawn permits — for a bull elk on the Salt Lake City unit. Don and his friends wanted to go along as spectators, not an easy thing to accommodate on an elk hunt, especially in the steep Wasatch Mountains east of Salt Lake Valley. There are no bleachers for this kind of spectating.

Way before dawn we parked near the Henefer road junction, near the city farm on Mount Dell creek. We must have spooked an elk herd which was feeding on the farm. When we turned off the car lights and our eyes adjusted to the dark we could see about fifteen elk lined out against the white snow on the bottomlands. Lynn spotted one animal that appeared to be larger than the others — a bull about fourth from the lead. It is characteristic of the elk herd to keep the breeding bull back in the lineup. The cows command the elk herd — and usually lead out wherever the herd goes. The bull is always somewhere back in the pack.

We could not shoot until daybreak. Nor could we risk killing a cow. So the herd was not harassed by any of us at that moment. We would wait until it got light and then hope to put on their tracks.

There was a foot of snow on level ground and hiking was hard. We did not track the first herd, but we positioned ourselves on various points in the event other hunters did as we did and put an elk herd to flight.

Don and his friends stayed at the road levels and walked the area for most of the day. Lynn and I trudged from ridge to ridge, hoping to scope a big bull and give our guests a chance to take home a rack of antlers and an elk hide, which we had promised them if we got an elk at all. One hunter with a cow permit got a good shot, and Don and Jack watched the animal brought off the mountain, dressed out, and taken away. At least this gave them the feel of an elk hunt.

All they took back to Hollywood this trip was a box of picked pintails. But that did not keep Don, Jack, and Verne away from Utah.

We staged an outing for them on Alva Dearden's land in Chalk Creek Canyon, Morgan County. Don had never hunted deer, and we got him a good bolt-action rifle for the occasion; we borrowed a gun that was not busy right then.

The night before we went out for the daybreak hunt I schooled Don well in the use of the bolt action, how to eject the shells, how to load, the safety features, how to sight in the rifle on a deer at two hundred yards, again at four hundred yards. We went through all the elementaries of the rifle use.

Maybe we over-schooled him.

Alva and Don positioned themselves on a ridge while several of us did some driving in their direction. Below them in the canyon a large buck had either been hiding or napping or chewing cud. When we came off the ridge the buck got up, walked out in plain view of the two hunters, and sniffed the landscape. Broadside it stood.

Seldom in one's lifetime of hunting does this dream target happen. He was not a running buck. He was too big and cautious to make a break into the open. He just stood there, seventy-five yards from Don and Alva.

Sportingly Alva whispered to Don to shoot. Don flipped off the safety and started bolting his rifle. He pumped five shells on the ground before he realized he had not pulled the trigger. Alva was just waiting for the deer to fall. Alva didn't have his gun handy for the backup shot. The deer bounced over the ridge and got away.

My fault. I hadn't told Don about pulling the trigger.

Once, in my early hunting days, I had thrown a single shell onto the ground in my excitement to kill an easy buck. But I had heard of someone unloading his five shots in the frantics of firing, and this day it really happened. Don was a good sport about it.

Another time with Alva Dearden, Don and Verne DeFore had a great hunt.

We had hunted Slaughter Hollow in Chalk Creek Canyon. Don had been doing some advertising for an automobile company, and they had provided him with a fancy station wagon, with a chrome rack on top, big air horns on the fenders. It was a fancy flivver, if ever I saw one. Don had especially chosen this car because of his forthcoming deer hunt in Utah.

En route to Chalk Creek, Don and his brother had stopped in Las Vegas to register for some of the deer hunt prizes. Contests were offered at several hotels in an effort to get hunters on their way to Utah to stop and spend some of their vacation cash on the gambling carpets. Don knew he was going into the Morgan mountains, where record deer had been taken. Some of the best mulies in the world were to be found there. This we had told him many times and he believed us — because it is true. With the right spread of antlers, Don and Verne could pick up $50,000 on their way back to

Hollywood. That would even beat advertising for automobile manufacturers.

On Don's arrival we were made aware of his registering for a record deer in Las Vegas. He wanted a big one, a record head, for that purpose.

Alva Dearden and Rulon Francis took Don in hand one day while the rest of us worked the draws and beat the brush. I liked to drive deer; it beat sitting on a ridge and just waiting for the runners. Stalking the deer was the best part of the program.

After we had made one drive down a favorite ravine (two deer had been felled) Rulon walked Don through some chaparral on the north slope. It was deep cover, and Rulon sensed a deer might be hiding in it. Rulon was right, and ahead of him an antler stuck above the brush. A huge buck lifted its head just enough for Don to get his shot. But the shot was high. It killed the deer but damaged the base of the skull where the two antlers are locked together. Bringing the deer off the mountain, the men broke the headbone and the antlers collapsed.

Around camp that night we did everything we could to position the antlers in their natural spread. We had a winner, we thought, but would anyone accept the normal position of the head when the base of the skull had been damaged and the antlers had fallen in?

Don would have had a winner with this rack, but the contest judges would not accept the broken head. Too bad. It could have paid the gasoline costs, at least.

We had set up a good camp at the spring where the deer usually trailed in for water and choice browse. Still eager to have a record head, Don decided to stay an extra day or two. The rest of us had to return to our work for another day and then would come back for a final day's hunting.

A storm was brewing in the west, and this concerned us. So we decided we would load up two big deer on the DeFore station wagon, and if the storm came they could come off the mountain and avoid the risk of remaining in deep snow.

The storm did come, and late at night the hunters decided to move out of the canyon. The road was rough, and although the deer were lashed solidly to the chrome rack, the first rut in the road caused the hunters some unpredicted stress. The roof of their fancy new station wagon caved in with the excessive weight of the deer. The automobile makers had made the top rack for reasonable luggage only. Four hundred pounds of deer, bouncing up and down with a rutted road, was not in the design plans of the car.

The hunters were able to drive the car out of the canyon, but only by sticking their heads out of the side windows. The deer were occupying most of the seat space. The men's faces were well washed by the storm by the time they reached the valley.

Don was certain the car would be replaced. He consoled himself with the thought that this was a good field test for the new model in station wagons. The only real problem they had was that 750-mile drive back to Hollywood. Like the smiling motorcyclist, they got a lot of bugs on their teeth.

And they laughed all the way home — they were the only hunters on the highway with deer so big that their car top caved in from the weight of their game.

And those big deer have grown bigger with their telling of this tale!

Who Put the Fish in the Trunk?

We had been fishing in the Greys River, from the top to the bottom — from where the sign on the trickle of a stream reads: "I am the Greys River. Watch me grow!"

And the river grows. And it offered us some fine sport that day.

But we had the Salt River in mind for late in the evening. Willard Bruce, Hy Hunsaker and Everett Thorpe knew the Salt River holes like they knew their own kitchen cupboards. They knew the big fish would bite just at dark and they would be big when they bit.

We were on the Salt River at the right time, with half a limit of Greys River fish and half a limit to go on the Salt River. Surely we would take a limit of these trout home! Take the big fish from the river and give the smaller ones a chance to grow up. That has always been my philosophy; and the fish culturists stand with me, for the most part.

This night we were after big fish — maybe one whopper each.

The three men with me spread out like a grass fire in a whirlwind, each having his favorite spot. I took whatever holes were left unfished.

As dusk settled thickly upon us I could hear fish splashing and fishermen grunting their approval or disapproval. Once in a while the silence of the night was broken with a little cussing — when the big one broke a line against the sunken stump.

I tied into a huge rainbow on a flatfish which I had weighed heavily for the swift current under the tree. It was getting so dark I could only read the stream by the sky's light upon it. The flatfish had double hooked the fish and turned the fish so it had more pulling power than if I could lead it directly from the mouth. This made it seem the larger.

I had made no contact with the other men, but I had heard them splashing a bit as they waded and walked from spot to spot. Several times they had gone to the car which was not far from our fishing place.

I had brought my car to the spot because I had to return to Salt Lake City that same night — had to be at the print shop the next day with my daily output. That monkey is always on a columnist's back, they say — the editor says.

My large rainbow trout just about filled me up, so I bid my colleagues goodnight and headed down the Star Valley road to Border, Evanston, and home.

It was starting another day when I unloaded my car to get the fish into the cooler. But there were more fish than I thought there should be. Covered with my sleeping bag and some newspapers were enough fish to feed a Boy Scout troop for months.

It had happened. Thorpe, Bruce and Hunsaker had dumped their fish onto me — said nothing about it. They would be in Wyoming a couple more days and would catch others.

Next day there were a lot of fish passed around the office.

I have wondered since that time what would have happened if I had been stopped in a police roadblock? Would anyone have ever believed my story?

I vowed that next time, when I went with these cagey culprits again, I would check my car trunk before I left them. Then I gave it a second thought. Might just leave the key in the latch again.

The Day We Lost the Little Fisherman

Ray Staley, Av Osguthorpe and several others of us had taken our young fishermen on a pack trip into the Wind River Mountains of Wyoming — packing out of the Pennock Trout Farm east of the Boulder Store. We wanted to give them a fishing trip to remember. Kenny Staley was seven years old.

Jerry Osguthorpe and Corey Miller were not much older. Brad Fisher was just a bit older than two colts we had taken along with eighteen horses. When Ray Staley staged a pack trip he went big. Twenty horses is big!

Whether the kids will remember it or not remained to be seen. But the fathers would — and have.

Crescent Lake was an ideal camp. There was horse feed aplenty. We could camp on a shelf overlooking the lake, with Bonneville Peak and other summit peaks of the Wind River Range as our backdrop. We could see the kids as they fished the lake — in the event one of them got pulled into the water by a record brook trout. And one of the world's largest brookies had been taken from Star Lake not far from Crescent Lake.

The fish were already nipping bugs from the surface when we started to unpack the horse train. I had been to the lake annually for several seasons and knew what to expect: pound-sized brookies which really liked kids — and their dads. They were rather easy to take.

We sensed that the kids were chafing at their tiny bits to get to the fishing. If we didn't get rods in their hands, some would soon be throwing rocks into the untouched lake — and we didn't want any rock throwing until we had our supper in the skillet.

Rather than have the little anglers underfoot while we were making camp, Av and I got the fishing rods set up as quickly as possible and one by one the young anglers trudged down the grassy slopes to the lake for those first casts. For the next half hour we heard nothing but fun talk, some thrill noises. Fish and kids got together pretty fast — and quite often.

Soon the young fishermen were talking about their totals — the number of brook trout they had lying in the grass where they were fishing.

"They must have fifty fish already," Ray said.

Fifty fish! We couldn't eat that many.

Instinctively, Av and several others went to the lake to

take a count, while others worked hard on supper as a lure to get the youngsters from their fishing spots. Yes, we had nearly fifty fish, and half of them hit the fillet board right then for the fry pan. Nothing like a fresh brook trout — even the ones which curl in the cooking. Better for the cook to let them cool overnight. But fresh fillets — you can't beat 'em.

After dinner we toasted some marshmallows and had a youth conference. We instructed the kids how to take the fish carefully from the hook and return them to the lake. They could keep only what they could eat. The young anglers got skillful at returning fish.

Three days of catching fish did not stop them from running to the lake before they had their shoes tied, or staying until the moon moved over the high rim to the east. They were sore at their arms, and after riding to about fifteen fishing spots they had a tender spot or two in the region of their hind pockets.

But they never lost their enthusiasm. Sometimes, when they saw pollywogs or chipmunks their attention was diverted. They lassoed a ground hog or two with a fly line, laying a loop over the hole and then waiting for the little rodent to stick his neck above ground. We had to clip a couple of leaders to free the captives.

When it came time to leave, we let the kids get in their last licks at fishing while we wrangled and packed the horses. We had enough fish to take out. From here on it was fishing for fun — and fun they had.

Came the head count, and we were missing two kids.

We found one at the lake, fishing behind a dwarf pine. Corey Miller remained missing, and inasmuch as he was one of four kids who belonged jointly to my wife and me I felt responsible to take him back home with us.

We organized a search and seizure party while Ray and Av tied the last hitches to the packs. We rode in different directions, agreeing to return within fifteen minutes. The next venture had an hour's limit.

I had gone along a small creek where the kids said Corey

had been fishing, and I saw some bear signs. Little boys, according to the legends of the high mountains, are bite-sized bits for big bruins.

We located the lad on this same stream. He didn't know we were waiting for him. Fishing for eight-inch brookies was superb, and he wanted no one to bother his fishing; so each time someone rode in his direction he hid behind the dwarfed cover until they passed. Like any honest angler, he wanted his privacy.

Delayed as we were, what do you say to a young man when he's doing only what comes naturally — like catching fish?

Going for the Golden Trout

Fishermen are fickle friends. Mention a new species of fish and the anglers go crackers to try for it.

I remember when they introduced the grayling in some of the Utah lakes — in the Murdoch Basin in the Uintah Mountains. Fish experts said it would be one year before they were catchable size. We waited that year, and the next one we were in the basin with our best flies.

We caught grayling. They were sporting, to say the least, but we had a pang of pity for the old standby trout, the rainbows and the cutthroats, and the browns and brooks, which had given us so much sport in years gone by. We felt as if we had forsaken our friends.

The same thing happened when news broke that the Wind River Range in Wyoming had some record California golden trout. Someone had caught a record-buster in Cook Lake, for instance, and there were more to be taken of that size or bigger. Around the Salt Lake City lunch tables we planned to go for the goldens — a new adventure, an excuse to get on the horses and ride the timberline trails of this beautiful part of our planet.

I contacted Lloyd Kenny of the Pennock Trout Farm near Boulder, Wyoming. Lloyd had bought the old trout farm and was using it for a packing outpost and dude ranch.

Lloyd too had been on the trail of the golden trout. He had taken some fishermen into Bonneville Lake, and they had caught some big ones — four pounds or so. That was news enough, and Enoch Eskelson and I were soon on our way to Bonneville Lake with Lloyd.

It was the hardest ride I ever had in the Wind River Range — up a brushy face where we had to lead the horses much of the way. The winds were wailing that day, and we hoped we could basin out and get some relief from the gale. That's why they call them the Wind River Mountains, Lloyd reminded us.

We had asked many people how to fish for goldens. Flies? Lures? Baits? The winds that day left us no choice. Put a fly in the air and it stayed there. So we shot heavy lures into the white-capping waters, hoping to find the big trout on the frantic feed for the smaller fish — which often happens when the winds lash the waters.

We had tied the horses downwind from some stub pines. We were right near timberline, and there was little relief from the forest growth. There was no time to allow an extra day for fishing. Like Lloyd Kenny said, you might wait out several years to find an un-windy day at Bonneville Lake. He had not known one, and he had been there half a dozen days trying for the red trout.

Clouds were forming above us, and with the peaks as a stopper we were soon in rain and sleet. We had come too far to cove up and let the rain have the area to itself. The time soon came when we could endure it no longer. We had not seen a fish nor a sign thereof. You didn't have to be very smart to know that we were not on time to take fish very often, if at all. We turned tail and left.

It had been a couple of years since Lloyd was at the lake. And most of the reports he had on golden trout were hand-me-down talk; some others had passed the story along, and there might have been some stretching of the truth — which is said to be characteristic of those who sport at fishing. Also someone might have read the map wrong, and Bonneville Lake perhaps was not the one with the big goldens in it. So we reasoned as the rains sopped us.

We also considered another factor — Lloyd was no fisherman, and he might have got his tales twisted.

It was good to get off the timberline that day — we felt like three little icebergs riding horses. I don't know how horses feel about such things, but they too should have had some joy in getting off the sleet-torn ridge that day.

Years have passed since that day, and at this writing I have never known anything more about goldens at Bonneville Lake. And I might never know. But of one thing I'm sure! Most days, anyone who goes to far-up Bonneville Lake will have a bend in his fly line — windy bend.

That is where the winds of the world meet.

On that trip we passed by many lakes and trailed along many streams. We had a keen eye open for golden trout. I had seen a few goldens and knew how easily they were to see along a lake's edge or in a shallow of a feeder stream. We found none, though we rode many miles off the blazed trails to watch for them.

Down the mountain we stopped at Rainbow Lake, where some of the area's largest trout have been taken. I learned about Rainbow Lake once when I met some sportsmen from Salina, Kansas. Each year they would fly from Salina to Pinedale, Wyoming, and pack into the highlands with Rainbow Lake as their base camp. "If you ever tell anyone about the big rainbows in that lake we will come to haunt you," one

*Joe Carter (left), Norm Tanner, and Enoch Eskelson pause by a lake
11,000 feet up in the Wind River Mountains.*

of them said, as he told how they had had the high lake almost
to themselves for many years — and had caught some noteworthy rainbow trout.

I promised to keep their secret, and as long as I was writing
a daily epistle for a newspaper I never gave their base the
spotlight. I believed that fishermen should find their own
good fishing holes; and we appreciated their telling us about
the big rainbow trout. We proved their story to be true as the
years came and went thereafter. They had fished every lake
on the west slope of the Wind River range and were knowl-
edgeable about the natural resources in that area.

We caught some three-pound rainbows on several trips —
nothing larger. Joe Carter and I one day turned some trout we
believed would have been in the five- to eight-pound class.
Joe and I had a pleasant day trying for the big ones. Enoch

Eskelson and Norm Tanner wanted to punch their way over the snow cornices on Hay Pass and took off early in the day to make the long and adventurous ride.

Joe and I elected to save our saddle seats for another day and try to trick some of those big fish the Kansans told us about. It was a pretty day to do it — almost sans wind. Also, Joe was learning to fly fish, and this would give him some on-the-job training time. Enoch and Norm would rather be on their horses — and they had waited a year (with a lot of map studies) to try Hay Pass and look into the river side to the east of the high range. But like Joe said, he could "horse around" in the Salt Lake Valley cutting corrals, but fly fishing like this came only once in a lifetime.

There was a fine riffle on the lake, so we got into a cove where we had a quarter wind in our favor to cast a long fly. The sun was hazed — a situation I prefer for midday fly fishing. It gives the fish better visibility, so I have always contended. The glare upon the water, even with an overcast sky, make us fish by the "feel" of it.

We started with sunken flies — just under the surface. We waited for the telltale swirl of the fish, always expecting the largest lunker in the lake to favor us with a strike.

I seldom fish two flies, an art my father taught me in his finest days (maybe to give a trout a selection and maybe to anchor one fly, the trailer, while you manipulated the other, the dropper). But this day I thought I would return to this ancient art and skitter the dropper fly as an added attraction.

The added attraction worked. Just as I was to lift the flies from the water for another cast, a huge rainbow swirled high in the water, almost out of it, and grabbed the dropper fly.

He not only grabbed the fly but he inherited it right then. The two-way effort, on the part of the pisces and the piscator, soon caused the parting of the two. The fish got my outfit, but only after I had a pretty good look at his breadth. He looked as broad as a barrel in that refractive light of the lake.

That was one of those famous fish the Kansans talked about.

Joe Carter, fishing not far from me, didn't see the fish but he heard the fishermen in the excitement of the moment. That one fish turned up the fever, and we lashed the lake harder than ever, hoping that one like him would soon show us how Rainbow Lake fish really fish.

And it happened.

Two-thirds of a good cast in distance a fish I couldn't see sucked in the trailer fly and turned toward the far shore. My fly reel had no drag set upon it (I never liked to play a fish by the drag), and I opened the reel and let it spin. The pull was so heavy I thought I had opted for an otter, a water critter I had seen often in the Wyoming wonderlands.

I tried to turn the big fish, or whatever it was, but only turned him from north by northeast to straight north. He wasn't turnable at that time. Since I had lost a big one once at Strawberry Reservoir for not having backing on my fly line, I had spooled plenty of spare line on all my reels. I was smug about my position right then. I figured the foe could take flight to the farthest nook of the lake and I still would have some contact with him. So I let the fish wander his own habitat.

When the tautness of the line made me think he had tuckered himself, I started to work the fish to my side of the fight. I looked for a gentle slope to bring him to shore, and having located a gentle slant of the shoreline I guided my adversary in that direction.

While all this was going on, Joe just kept fishing. For the few previous days he had fevered with the technique of fly fishing, which he was learning fast. He didn't pause to peek upon my prize fish as it neared the shallows.

The fish sensed it was being led to its doom and made a struggle to get to the deeper water, and I let it have this last lap. That was my mistake. It exploded for a final fling into the air and snapped my leader.

At first I was in the pain of defeat. I wanted to show Joe what a real big rainbow looked like. I also wanted to show Norm and Enoch that we did not lose out completely that day by declining their invitation to ride over Hay Pass.

Then I was consoled by the defeat. The fish, a gallant one, had won the struggle. He had the hook in his lip but would shed that shaft of steel in less than a day.

Joe and I had seen the sheen of the fish's side as the rainbow bowed in his last leap. It would weigh five pounds, we told our horsebacking buddies as we supped around the pine fire that evening. Joe and I might have bored them with our tall tales. Actually, Norm and Enoch had had more of a day, experiences counted, than Joe and I had. We had missed some excitement, as we learned after our fish stories were related.

Near Hay Pass, Norm and Enoch, staying with the snow-drifted trail, so they thought, had one of their horses break through the snow near the lake's edge. The horse went down with its legs virtually hanging in the rocks. It had no power to lift itself out of the pit, so the two horsemen unsaddled the gelding and started to hand-dig the snow to free it. It took more than an hour before the horse could be rolled out of the hole to a spot where it could get a footing. Then the shoreline ice fractured as the horse panicked, and the horse was soon in the lake with a splash.

Instinctively it swam from the snow pack to a small island that was not frozen. It stood on the rocks, after shaking itself somewhat, and left the fishermen ashore with two saddles, one horse, and a heck of a problem.

How does one get a horse to get into icy waters? Half the lake was frozen — only the section where the island was was clear of ice. The horse had to make its own decision to swim. There was no way to get to the horse, nor to prod it into the water.

For years Enoch had been a friend of his horse. They had made many mountain excursions together. There had been some rough times. Now Enoch talked to his horse as one fisherman talks to another. The horse understood as Enoch beckoned him from the rock pile into the water. While Enoch and Norm cleared a place for the horse to come ashore through the deep snow, the horse swam his part of the lake.

The saddle was soon on and the return to camp began.

That alone took some of the frostbite and cold water treatment out of the party. The horse was walked most of the way. It turned up lame from a rock bruise that came when horse and rider fell into the snow pit.

The fact that it was the warming part of July helped to cure the cools of the entire party, including the horse.

After listening to the Hay Pass explanation our fishing day seemed unimportant. It hardly mattered that we caught several rainbows in the two-pound class, and ate them that night almost without comment. Somehow we were glad to have our horse back. Having a saddle on your own hands in that high country, with no horse to carry it, can be a problem.

I recalled around the fire that night how a friend of mine, Wib Dangerfield, found himself in that predicament in these same Wind River Mountains when his horse left him one night, and after days of searching the horse could not be found. Wib laughed often about how cumbersome a horseless saddle can be when you're that far from a pickup truck.

They Should Name It Skunk Hollow

There is a place near Ken Rogerson's place on the Weber River which he has dubbed Miller Gulch. Misnamed it is; it should be called Skunk Hollow.

For several years, on the last day of the hunting season, Ken and I, and sometimes some others, would stage a last hunt on top of Mill Hollow, near Mud Flat. Some days we hoped we wouldn't kill a deer. Other days we wanted to. Ken

Rogerson, a fine friend and true man of sport, always saw to it that I rode his favorite horse, old Skunk.

I don't know why they named a pretty gelding like that Skunk. Maybe it was done out of flattery — he had a feathered star on his forehead that looked like a polecat's pelt.

One year, before dawn, on the last day we were on top of the mountain eyeing every point. The horses knew the trail to the top. They had gone that route many times that week.

It isn't easy for two men to make a drive in that expansive timberland. But Ken knew all the tricks. He chose the small canyons. He knew the deer trails — and which way the deer would move when they were moved at all.

Ken chose to rim the aspen area. I was to go down the other side of the ravine to a point where I could see the trail coming down. There I was to tie Skunk and take position in the timber in the event a deer came that way.

Ken's instructions were detailed. I reviewed them with him.

"Never mind," Ken said. "Skunk will go to the tree where he's to be tied. You just drop the reins and go back about twenty-five yards and sit where you can eye the trail that comes into the dip."

Skunk did it all, finally stopping near a tree. I wheeled out of the saddle, walked back twenty-five paces, and there was a spot where I could see the trail coming off the rim. But it was a close view and I was no more than forty yards from the trail.

I waited silently. Soon I heard that wonderful noise of the crackling of aspen boughs.

Cautiously a large buck came down the trail and paused at the exact spot Ken told me it would.

Skunk didn't flinch when I shot. The deer fell on the trail. I waited for Ken, and by the time he arrived I had the deer dressed out, gamble branch spreading its brisket, and snow-cooled.

"Now we'll go down the Chokecherry trail," Ken said. "This is a good drive and we need one deer. A big buck, if possible. You follow the trail, and when you get to the rock

Ken Rogerson, left, with Hack Miller on Ken's trained deer horse,
Skunk.

outcropping you take the right fork and rise on the rim where
you can cover the entire face of the mountain across the
canyon. It's a good spot."

Again there were some details I wanted reviewed — to be
sure I didn't foul up the action.

"Best way," Ken concluded, "let Skunk take the rein. He
knows the trail and where to take you."

At that point I was feeling somewhat that this was Skunk's
hunt and not mine. The horse took me to the spot, stopped,
seemingly went to sleep. I took position on the point, scoped
the sidehill, waited.

In due time Ken came into view, and I mounted Skunk.
Skunk took me to another place, stopped; I dismounted and
went to the nearby point, sat down, scoped the hill while
waiting for Ken to show again. Methodically, I mounted

Skunk and he trudged along the rim and waited in the pass until Ken came up through the aspens.

Same routine going down the canyons on the north side en route back to the Rogersons' house on the Smith and Morehouse stream. Each time Skunk took the side trail, paused, then moved on.

It was a little like riding the Disneyland frontier, where everything goes according to the control boards. But I liked it. I got a beautiful buckskin, had a pleasant day afield, did none of the planning, and little of the execution of the plans.

Ah, Skunk! What wonderful times we have had together in some of the world's wonderlands! What more can a hunt in the hills offer any human?

Fishing Ike Walton's English Streams

I went into Dave Zinik's sporting goods store to say good-bye to my old friend. Dave and I had seen a lot of sporting years together — in hunting and fishing affairs, softball leagues, basketball sponsorships, etc. Now I was headed overseas in World War II; my turn to take the big ship to the conflict in Europe.

Dave asked if I needed a compact fishing rig in the event I got cornered and had to live off the land. A new thought — fishing in Europe. Maybe I could decoy as an innocent angler and thereby gain an advantage on some enemy. Or at any rate just fish for fun. I accepted the rig — a small saddle rod, some reel and line, and some catgut leader material.

The time did come when I could introduce the English streams to the Colorado spinner. It wasn't exactly legal, but then neither was a world war, and I wasn't getting paid too much to trifle with such trivia. I figured that England wouldn't grudge me a cast or two in the River Test or River Trent, where Izaak Walton once fished and of which he so endearingly wrote in *The Compleat Angler*.

I guess I was the first Yankee to introduce a spinning blade to the big browns in the leased fishing waters in southern England. If so, it is about my only "first," and each person, I reason, is entitled to a first.

My assignment as Transportation Officer in England right after invasion day was to bring army and air force convoys to the south ports for embarkation to the European operation. As I marshalled the forces and their vehicles for loading, I came across much interesting landscape in the south part of England where Izaak Walton spent so many pleasant seasons afishing.

I coveted his streams, and sometimes I stopped a jeep or motorcycle, whichever I was using at the time, on a nearby bridge to ogle the waters for bug-snatching trout. Some days, as some of those three-pound brown trout in leased or private waters rose for a lazy cahill fly, I suffered to think I could not apply a little American technique to this stream or that fishing spot.

One day it was more than I could take, and I had put in my motorcycle saddle bag a small fishing rod, attached to which was a Colorado spinner. I found a holly bush where I could secrete my motorbike and hug close to the stream at a point where there was a big hole against the bank.

Looking in both ways to see that the gendarmes were not sighting their rifles at me, I made a cast across the stream and let the spinner "work" against the big stump which had turned the water's course. A monster trout moved upon the spinner and I set the hook.

In those days we used catgut for leader material, and this leader had not been pre-soaked — hadn't been wetted since it left Dave Zinik's sporting goods store. The leader broke quickly, with hardly much of a tug. But I saw the big brown trout broadside. I was glad I didn't have the fish on when a British lorry came down the road. As it was I stayed under cover, like a thief in a berry patch, until the British vehicle drove by.

I had no more leader material and no more spinners with me. But that was all right. I had proved my point. A brown trout is a brown trout, no matter which flag he bites his bait under.

I wanted to make a second cast in that river, but I never got around to it again.

Besides, poaching trout in English waters, even though we were allied in a common cause, was not sporting. Having proved my point, I telescoped my rod into an abbreviated length, tied it to the bike's baggage rack, and headed back to my work.

I might not have been so sporting if I had had another Colorado spinner right then.

Apparently some American soldiers were faced with a similar temptation. Not long after my incident with the brown trout, the bobbies (police) contacted me at headquarters and told me that some of "your Yanks" had dynamited a choice fishing water near Dorchester and killed many fish, and that the United States would be billed for the loss of the trout.

It just happened that some GI saw a few big trout in a deep hole in one of the trout streams, and using his training in the effects of a hand grenade he pulled the pin and let the "pineapple" explode in the hole. The fish came to the top fast, and the GIs gathered them up and went their way. The fact that they left the little ones gave the bobbies the clue of the fish take.

Of course, we paid the bill.

I have often wondered if I would have had to pay for one trout if that catgut leader hadn't broken when I turned the big one.

That, at least, would have been the sporting thing to do.

Star Lake

When a twelve-pound brook trout was taken from Wyoming's Star Lake the fishing world's attention was turned in that direction.

Surely there would be a bigger brookie than that — and one maybe which would top the world record held by Dr. W. J. Cook — a fourteen-pound, eight-ounce brook trout taken from Ontario's Nipigon River in 1916. Some of those ancient records have proved to be more fiction that fact, but the only way to take them from the record books is to record a bigger fish.

Here was hope — Star Lake, along the highline trail of the Wind River Mountains, up the trail from the Boulder Creek drainage. We had been in the Wind River for a week, with Dr. Y. D. (Enoch) Eskelson, Joe Carter, and Norm Tanner. Star Lake was on our agenda. This was down the mountain in the grazing district, where we could freshen the horses with better feed for a day or so — and try for a world-record brook trout.

We arrived at Star Lake midafternoon, and after making camp we set out for the record quest. We saw a dead lake right then and decided to do what we could to arouse the fish with some good action lures.

We started on the shallow side of the lake because we could wade it. Everything was wrong. The sun was burning down upon the lake, and we knew no self-respecting brookie would be basking in that intense heat. There was no bug hatch upon the surface. It was dead. The only riffle was the one we made.

Far out in the middle of the lake a couple of big square-tails, as brook trout are often called, broke water. We knew they were big fish. Big fish make more motion than little fish. I needed a boat or a raft or some water wings to get to them. I vowed right then that someday I would return with a collapsible boat and go for those middle-of-the-lake beauties.

Joe Carter holds onto a big one at Star Lake in the Wind River Mountains of Wyoming.

We broke for a bite to eat. Norm and Enoch had fixed some food, and Joe and I sat around the fire with an eye toward the lake. Slowly as the sun sank in the pines we could see the trout move closer to where we wanted them to be.

Joe had caught the fly-fishing fever and was burning hot to get to the lake. His casting was rather limited but he was trying, and if we could get him into one of those big brooks I knew I would have a fly-fishing devotee for the rest of his life. It was turning cold as we waded barefoot into the sandy shallows of the lake, across the lake from the inlet.

I had learned long ago that if you are going for record fish you have to have a habitat which will support them. I reasoned that a fourteen-pound brookie would need a couple pounds of feed every half day to "grow him" to record size. And he couldn't get that much feed from nipping gnats from the lake's surface. For this reason I hated to give up the bigger lures, the fatteners, for the little nymphs and dry flies the shoreline fish were feeding on.

The bug hatch came on strong with the darkening day, and the wind was right at our backs, blowing the surface feed onto the lake and allowing us to get the most distance in our fly casting.

I kept some big streamer flies ready for the dark hours of the night. I remembered the Alaskan brown bear and how, as a member of the grizzly family, he reached record size because he had the spawning salmon to feed upon. His brother, the grizzly, remained normal size because he had to find his food on the ant hills, on the berry bushes, and on the grub worms in the rotting timber. Then there was the kamloop rainbow which had reached record size in Idaho's Lake Pend Oreille. Kamloops were just a rainbow. But the kamloop had an advantage with the abundance of nine-inch blueback salmon that were in the lake. This provided the rainbow all the food it could absorb and brought it to record weight of thirty-six pounds in four years. Take such food away from a fish and you have the normal size — and quickly.

While I was explaining all this to Joe as we stood knee deep in the lake, it came to my mind that if there were fourteen-pound brookies in this lake they would have to do their foraging for food at night — when the little fish had little defense against them. I told Joe that no matter how cold it got and how painful the cold water was upon our legs, we would have to stay deep into the darkness and give the shoreline fishing a good try. He agreed.

As we planned our piscatorial approach the fish came close enough to reach if we could cast a seventy-five-foot fly. I gave it my best effort but could not reach the feeders. It was a reef they were feeding on — maybe the best food in the lake. I walked to shore, stripped off my Levi's and returned to the lake. I would go half in, and if that didn't work the shirt would be next to go. We had to get to the fish. Joe stripped down too. On the first cast I had a fish. I asked Joe for help and he waded it ashore while I took his rod and made the longest cast I could make and hit into another. Nice four-pounders they were. As nice a brook trout as I ever looked upon.

Joe just couldn't get far enough with his fly to be among the feeders. But one did come too close and liked Joe's upright fly as it fluttered on the surface. There was a tremendous splash as the fish took Joe's line almost to the core of the reef. Never had fish and man had more disagreement. That was the maddest brook trout I ever saw. And there was never a happier fisherman than Joe when he finally led the spent fish to shore. Joe could have been sitting stark naked on an iceberg during that time and never known it. Quickly he was back in the water, waist deep, with his shirt tail tied in a square knot as high on his chest as he could tuck it.

Joe and I laid in a dozen of these dandies and admired them each time we added another brookie to the bunch. These were our take-home fish. They were worth showing, or hanging on the wall in a man's den.

Darkness set in and we quit for suppertime. Then we were at it on another section of the lake, still believing there was a big brookie prowling the shoreline in search of the finger-lings.

No luck! And after trying everything in the tackle box we quit.

Enoch and Norm had tried their hand at fishing when they saw what fun Joe and I were having. They caught a few — all of them were some of the best brookies we had ever taken. But this wading out in your bare skins to catch another fish was not for them. They sat around the campfire and listened to Joe and me chatter about the fun we were having.

They left a little fire, and to thaw out before hitting the sack Joe and I got a blazer going. There is an old Indian saying: "White man build big fire and sit far back; Indian build little fire and sit close." Joe and I built a white man's fire and sat close like an Indian that night.

We planned an early departure for the Toboggan Lakes trail to Lloyd Kenny's place on Pennock Trout Farm, a spur off the main Boulder Creek road. This is where we had left our trucks and trailers. Then we were to drive to Salt Lake City that same day. This meant that if Miller and Carter were to take with them a world-record brook trout it had to be caught before breakfast that morning.

The sky hadn't even begun to golden up in the pine forest to the east when I slipped out of the bag, grabbed my rod, and went to the lake.

Not a movement anywhere.

I tried spinning gadgets and the flies. Nothing worked.

The other men were stirring around the campfire, doing the necessary chores. I got guilty in the conscience and conceded victory to any of the world-record brookies that might be in Star Lake.

On the ride down the Toboggan Lakes trail to Lloyd Kenny's place, we reflected upon our pleasant eight days in the Wind River mountains. Where else could you seek world-record golden trout one day and world-record brook trout the next? And where else could you spend your other time in the glacier basins in the timberline country? Our rides over Hailey and Washakie passes were memorable treks, and our stay at Pyramid Lake, with no one near us for three days, was a pleasant time for us.

As for Joe and me, we would return each year to Star Lake. There must be a record somewhere in that beautiful lake. If not, we shall at least have the fun of thinking there is.

Two-Gun Goose Shooter

Lynn Hansen had cased the goose flight thoroughly at the Chesapeake Gun Club. He had been watching for a week and after the geese had gone each morning he had gone to the area and expertly dug some goose pits.

Then he invited me to go help him kill a goose. I went.

We were in the blinds when day broke. Several others were also going to be in selected positions.

But the others couldn't find the pits in the dim of dawn, and Lynn, gracious gentleman that he was, got out of his cover and went to the pits to show his friends.

He got them located all right just as he heard the honkers honk overhead. The flight was up and coming — from a couple miles away.

If he ran for the blind he would spoil the hunt for all of us.

He hit the grain stubble and lay still, yelling to me that his gun was ready and telling me to use it. That way I could get six shots into the flight, if I could work it right — get a gooser for him.

The geese set their wings and came in. I got one dead and one dying, emptying one gun quicker than I should have and grabbing Lynn's gun in an attempt to get another round of Canadians. I could think of no law against helping another hunter out in an emergency such as this.

It turned out badly. Instead of taking three good shots I took six bad ones — we got one goose each when we should have had a goose each for the oven on Thanksgiving Day, Christmas and New Year's Day.

Lynn Hansen was one of the best shooters I ever knew. He could fell a pheasant or down a duck as quickly as anyone.

I stationed myself one day in a secret blind. I wanted to photograph Lynn knocking big ducks out of the sky. I took twelve camera shots, but Lynn didn't hit a bird for my camera. Never had I seen him miss twelve in a row — or even one in a row, for that matter.

We got the boat and he said he was going to the clubhouse. I assumed he was offended. We left the decoys where they were and went in. "My barrel's bent and I have to straighten it," Lynn said, as he put his gun to the vise and had me help him tug on the butt of the barrel.

He looked down the barrel and said it was okay, and we went immediately back to the barrel blind.

I set up the camera again. He hit the next twelve birds — I got some of the greatest duck pictures I ever took.

If it had merely been reported to me, I would have taken all that barrel-bending with a grain of salt. But I was there to see what happened. And it did!

He Won His Own Trophy

Lincoln White was one of the co-owners of Bullfrog Basin on Lake Powell. Bullfrog, Hall's Crossing, Wahweap — all of them were competing for attention in those first days of the lake. It meant business for them. Linc knew he had to get fishermen interested in the Utah end of the lake, and big bass were the attention-getter. Some big bass were being taken in the Bullfrog area. The upper waters of the lake, as the impounded waters sought a higher level, were the best attraction for the angler.

Linc conceived the idea of a fishing tournament — a monthly prize and a season award. He had some fancy plaques fashioned for the contest, and one day, when he decided to deliver the hardware, he asked me to go along. In good time Linc had his business matters at the lake managed and we headed uplake to some of our favorite fishing holes.

Knowles Canyon had exceptional rocks in it, the kind bass like to sulk behind. There never was a better bass hole anywhere. We took live salamanders along in the event we had to stoop to baiting for the bass. That was a last resort for bass pluggers.

We caught fish, all we wanted. We lingered in those large rocks, most of them with straight edges — they had fallen from the overhanging sandstone walls in cube-shaped pieces the size of some houses. Plugging was excellent fun, and the bait stayed in the bucket.

That first canyon on the north side of Knowles was our hot spot. Before rising water obliterated it from surface view there was a large pyramidal rock far enough from shore to form a mecca for monster largemouth bass. I could drift into it without oar or motor — from its blind side.

Linc stood poised for the one cast — just over the top of the rock. It would be a blind cast to the shaded side. We couldn't see what happened when Linc's plug smacked the surface. It sounded like an alligator splashing in the shallows. Linc's line tightened; his rod bent and the star drag of the spinning reel sang the pretty song.

The fish, at first, swam hard away from the rock and then turned to it as the drag on the reel forced him to do. He sulked under the rock long enough for the helmsman to manage to free himself so he could let Linc fight the fish on the open side.

It was a good fight with four-pound line. Linc disciplined himself artfully. This one he didn't want to lose, especially after Linc and his fish looked eye-to-eye as the bass tried to lift its hulk high above the water line.

I never carry a net in my boat — too much tangle — and who wants fish that badly? Waterskiers don't like nets in their tow boats. Besides, I never owned one. So Linc had to gill the bass if he was going to get it into the boat at all. In due time, when the fish opened its big mouth, Lincoln grabbed it. Linc could have rammed his forearm down that throat — to the elbow. Never have I seen such a cavity on a fish.

The bass and Linc, like two fighters in their corners, calmly gasped for air. It didn't matter that the wind had drifted us into the rocks; I had to admire this fish. It weighed over eight pounds.

Linc won the monthly prize, and at year's end he claimed the big one.

Like I told him, he should have left the hardware home in the first place.

That Unusual Provo River Trout

We were floating the Middle Fork of the Salmon River in 1946 for the fun of it. No dudes this time. No records to set. No history books to write. We just wanted to float a river for the fishing, the scenery, the thrill of whipping the white waters.

There were four of us: Dr. Russell G. Frazier of Bingham Canyon; Frank Swain of Copperton; Dave Curry of Vernal; and me. Each had a five-man rubber raft, a left-over, or a spill-over, from World War II, which had just ended.

Actually, Frank, David, and Dr. Frazier had waited for me to finish my five-year army stint, and this trip was my welcome-home party. And it was a welcome trip. There was no one else on the river. It was much the same as we left it in 1939, and again when Doc and Frank left it in 1936, when they were the first rivermen to run the Middle Fork's full course. And with those new-fangled rubber rafts, this was like riding a magic carpet in comparison to the old wooden boats we used before the war.

We were on time for the big salmon run — the Chinooks or Kings which came up each year from the Pacific Ocean, and which laid their eggs, or fertilized them (in the male's case), and then died in the river. We had taken with us the finest salmon fishing gear we could assemble.

At Sulphur Creek we went upstream to find the spawners, and we found them. We could catch all the fish we wanted. They were on every riffle to spawn. Some were not as old and beaten and bruised as others. We picked some good fish, caught them on eggs, spinners, lures. They really were not feeding — just more curious about the baits, we reasoned.

I shan't forget that day. Several miners were camped near the confluence of Sulphur Creek and the Middle Fork, a flat place where we have stayed many times since that date. They said they could use some fish if we caught extras. We caught extras.

We had several miles to walk back to our boats, and that meant packing half a dozen big salmon, averaging about twenty-two pounds. We tied them by their tails to a pole pine and then shouldered the pine and started down the river trail. We kept in step, and this caused the fish to sway; and in short time we had sore shoulders where the pole pine rubbed us. We abandoned this mode of freighting, and tied the tails of two fish together and slung them over our shoulder.

I could carry four salmon handily, heavy as they were. They fit snugly against me as I sauntered down the edge of the stream. But there was a problem. The flies started to gather around me, and eventually I had to have a good scrub down in the sulphur spring at the campground — what we called the old Fuller Place.

We saved one of the best salmon for our dutch oven feast that night and gave four of the others away.

Frank had promised to show his young fishermen at home what a big salmon was like, so he decided to keep one — the biggest. When some of our river friends saw the salmon Frank kept for himself they called it a "dog" salmon. It had large teeth, like fangs on a dog. It was a little out of species with the handsome Kings. It was just a big, ugly salmon of some species or other. They told us they called it a dog salmon because it was fit only for the dogs. Another expert said it was so ugly it looked like a dog with those fangs, and so it was called a dog salmon.

I had the balanced load, so I volunteered to carry the fish on the prow of my rubber raft. At night we hung the critter up to cool, and for the day's river run we wrapped it in heavy tarps. It got smelly after a few days, but I tried to keep it downwind from me so I could enjoy the fragrance of the Ponderosa forests. By the time we reached the end of the river run where the Middle Fork meets the main Salmon River, the fish was pretty ripe.

Frank did show it to his family. But his wife insisted it be disposed of quickly.

Frank owned a cabin on the Provo River just downriver from Deer Creek Reservoir damsite. With a bit of play he placed the huge fish, about a twenty-seven-pounder, alongside the river on the grassy bank, where it would surely be found. He had picked a trafficked trail by Vivien Park where many fishermen tried their tricks on the big trout in the bridge hole. In due time (and in this case due time was short time) the huge fish was discovered.

Someone called the newspaper (not mine) and told about the fish. Stories were written about it. Some argued it was a cross between a German brown trout and a cutthroat. One said it looked like a huge channel catfish without the catfish head — the fish was a hybrid catfish with good looks. The conservation officers had their say too. Each person had an opinion.

Frank telephoned this reporter and told me what he had done. I remained silent.

The fish had spoiled. It could not be salvaged. But it could be given the usual postmortems.

If you have heard about the legend of the whopper trout at Vivien Park, that's the story.

It wasn't a dirty trick at all. Consider how many people have since tried their luck in this hole, hoping to find another like it.

"I Know I've Forgotten Something"

It had been a great day on the old Chesapeake Gun Club with Lynn Hansen, Leo Capson, Del Stoker, Bim Meyers and others.

I was Leo's guest this hunt, and after we had filled up we decided to head out for home and have dinner at Maddox Cafe in Brigham City rather than wait for the Alice Davis meal at the clubhouse. Alice cooked the best ducks in the world, but we decided to pass up the Davis ducks this time and head for the Salt Lake shed.

We put guns away, kenneled Leo's dog, put the boat in the boat house and fixed the motor, stacked the decoys — did everything we should have done.

Maddox meals in Brigham City were famous, and as the sun set over the lake at the west Cappy and I ate heartily. But there was something bothering Cap. He was sure he had forgotten something.

The cream pie for dessert had just been brought to our window table when Cappy snapped his fingers and sighed quite in shame. "I left Art Moore in the duck blind," he confessed. "I was supposed to go get him when we quit and bring him with us. He's still out there in the barrel waiting for us."

Cream pie notwithstanding, Cappy dashed to the phone and cranked into the club. He explained the situation to B. W. Heard, who let Cappy suffer a little before explaining. "We got him all right. We watched you go in and then figured someone was supposed to get Art, so we checked on him. He's on his way home with some of the other hunters."

Cappy and I searched for an excuse; but we couldn't find one. We just forgot dear old Art.

A hunter would never leave his dog in the duck blind. But other hunters? Well . . .

And that is what bothered Leo Capson all the way home that night.

They Called Him "Chub" Turnbow

No one could fish the Strawberry Reservoir with fly rods better than Dave Wright of Midway and Bill Turnbow of Heber.

They were scientific in their quest for bug-biting biggies. Both had cabins near the lake near the Dave Madsen camp. From their front windows they could, with power scopes, scan the surface to watch for the top-feeders. And if they found feeders in the fever they would even leave their ham and eggs in the skillet and run for their boats.

One day, for instance, Dave was scanning the east shoreline. He stopped his truck long enough to talk to one of the shoreline fishermen who was baiting from that part of the eastern beach.

"Haven't seen anything but a school of carp swim by," the angler told Dave.

Carp?

"Which way did they go?" Dave asked.

The man pointed south down the shoreline and said, "They're not very far away and they're swimming that way."

Dave hurried to his truck and sped down the lake road.

Yep, there they were — a school of large cutthroats feeding the surface, sucking in the surface bugs as they cruised not far from the shoreline.

Dave got ahead of them and was well out with his fly-rod casts when the fish came to him. He caught three big fish out of that "school" of trout. That was his fishing for the time. His search ended right there. Another day there would be another surface search — and maybe some of that big-time action on a willowy fly rod — action which no fishermen, anywhere in this planet, can match.

It was along this same east shoreline that, while I was fishing with Dave and Bill, we got into some feeders.

Usually we trolled the old Strawberry wobblers until we spotted some bug-nipping natives. Then we would put up the trolling rods and go into action with the fly rods.

One day we saw a monster of a cutthroat trout heading our way, some fifty yards out from the boat.

Three of us got down in the boat, sitting on the boat's bottom to keep the lowest profile possible.

"He's coming your way," Bill said, as he watched the dorsal fin of the big fish surface and then submerge into the water. "He's a big one. You'll have to cast about ten feet in front of him. Then set your feet for a fight — because you'll have just that."

Just as Bill told me, I cast ahead of the fish — there was a "V" wave as the big fish swam fast for the fly. I set the hook as the fish swirled.

And then the reel sang that beautiful tune as the fish swam hard away from the boat and the line cut the water — as if I had hooked a sailfish.

My first thought was how I would stop that fish from taking all the line off my reel. I had not heeded Dave's advice, earlier in the season, when he told me to spool on two hundred feet of backing line — as a safeguard measure. I had about one hundred feet of fly line. That was soon gone. Just as I was watching the bare spool show on the reel, I thumbed the reel and let the fish break the leader. In this sacrificial effort I lost the fish but saved my fly line. And I broke Dave's heart when he saw what had to be done because I had not done as he suggested.

Bill got a good look at the fish. He estimated it at about fifteen pounds.

Next day I had backing on my fly reels — all of them. And I have never hooked a fish that big since.

At Dave's cabin one day Bill and I decided to make a fast run to the east shoreline for a little pre-breakfast fly fishing — in case the big trout were eating on the early bug hatch at sunrise. Dave decided to watch us with his glasses and have breakfast ready when we came in. Then, the plan was, we would troll the lake while searching for the feeding trout — the fly-fishing schools.

Bill cranked up the old Evinrude motor and we sped to the east side — to hit the choicest waters where the bugs might be blowing off the sagelands onto the lake.

Nothing hit our Brig Mitchell spoons as we headed for Salamander Bay. Unusual winds blew hard upon us, and we didn't realize how bad they were in the comforts of the bay. Hoping for a break with the wild winds, we stayed in the quieter waters. In the approaching storm there was no way we could cross the main part of the lake and get back to the cabin. Dave would have to eat all the pancakes and eggs he had prepared.

We fished from the dam to Joe Bush. Several times we measured the winds with the thought that we might chance a return to the cabin. But Bill figured we could make out. He knew the camp tender at the sheep camp just up the side of the sagebrush knoll. We could stop in for some sourdoughs there — eat with his friend. Dave would understand why we hadn't come in.

No fishing luck, and as the hours passed we hoped the fish would turn on. But storms on the Strawberry have their way of calming the fish.

When we finally decided to go for the feed bag at the sheep camp, we found no sheep camp. It had been moved several miles down the valley — to keep with the sheep. No sour-doughs. And increasing winds.

We just trolled the safer waters; we tried every trick in the tackle box.

Finally Bill got a hit, and we savored it as something of a

miracle. The fish fought vigorously. Bill guessed it would weigh under three pounds. Bill said it was definitely a cutthroat, because it preferred to stay deep and fight a cutthroat fight.

It turned out Bill had snagged a one-eyed chub in the rump — just above the tail. That accounted for the stubborn battle the fish offered. We netted the chub — mostly to remove it from the lake. Chubs were a disaster fish at that time.

It was midafternoon when we docked and returned to the cabin. Dave chuckled when he saw Bill's chub.

Thereafter, as one would guess, it was "Chub" Turnbow.

While the Game Wardens Watched

It was really too early to ride horses into timberline country. Word was out that the trails were still snowpacked in places, even on July 1, 1950.

That would make the adventure more interesting, we reasoned.

Avaron Osguthorpe was a veteran horseman — a veterinarian, in fact. He loved to be in the saddle. And he knew what horses could do, in snow or on dry trail.

We couldn't think of a reason why we should not ride into the Uintah Lake country. In checking with Lou Monk at the Hades Canyon Ranch we learned there was deep snowpack in places, but Lou thought we could make it. The warning only made the trip more intriguing. We could always turn back — but that would take some pretty rough riding.

We found the trails as Lou Monk said they would be, but we rode around the snow. The sunspot campgrounds at

Grandaddy Lake were dry, and the grass was nibblin' tall for the horses. And we had taken oats with us just in case. The first night we established that fish could be caught rather easily. Nothing big — they just fit a fry pan.

We had packed lightly so we could move, ride the country whenever and wherever it pleased us. Avaron was a horse-man who liked to sit in the saddle to ogle the scenery. He always wondered what was over the next ridge and the next one after that. We rode over a lot of ridges.

At Betsy Lake, not far from the big lake, we had the best fishing. And we noticed as we were about to ride into the Mohawk and Pine Island country that someone had been at Betsy Lake ahead of us. Fresh signs were everywhere.

We hadn't paid much attention to signs along the Hades Canyon trail. Maybe a fishing party had come down the Duchesne River from Mirror Lake, or up from the Rock Creek drainage from the Davies Ranch, and had come west by way of Fern Lake and Lodgepole Lake. It didn't matter. You can't be the first everywhere.

We noted where several horses had been tied to the trees near the little stream that ran into Grandaddy Lake. We saw some blood on the snow where something had been cached. This made us curious. We tracked around and noted there were many footprints near the lake's inlets. Also there were barricades across the small stream, rock piled up to stop the stream.

"Poachers," Av said, as it dawned on both of us that someone had made a haul on the spawners that had come from the big lake into the creeks to lay their eggs and perpetu-ate their kind.

We tied up and walked the small creek. Yes, someone had taken a lot of spawners. Every thirty feet or so the small creek had been impounded to make hand-catching the spawning trout easier. Poachers had used the snow banks here and there along the creek to keep the fish cool, or to hide their catch in case someone came upon them.

I got my camera from the saddlebag and took pictures as

Av broke up some of the small damsites to free the fish — allow them to return to the lake. Light was dull, so I had Av take one of the larger spawners (about sixteen inches long and no more than a pound in weight) to a sunny spot where we could photograph the condition of the trout. Spawners at that altitude are exceptionally gaunt. It was certainly no fish for the fry pan.

Carefully Av put the native trout back into the waterway and urged it to swim downstream — toward the lake. Its summer place was no more than seventy-five yards away. We could have carried it, and the others, that distance. Rather, we just took about an hour and cleaned the stream of its barricades so the fish could return in their natural way.

As we returned to our horses, two men rode up. A couple of friends, they were. Dick Goodworth and Guy Bronson had been patrolling this area for decades, watching over our natural resources as game wardens for the Utah Fish and Game Department. Many times I had ridden this range with them on patrolling trips or to haul fingerling fish into the high lakes in milk cans — prior to the days of airplane planting programs.

These men were on a stakeout. They knew spawners were being poached and hauled out of the country in sackloads. With their glasses they had scoped all our activities. But they couldn't figure why we didn't take the fish, after spending so much time in the small stream. Like Dick said, "We thought we had you nailed to the barn door on this one. But I guess we got the wrong men."

We all walked up the small creek to be sure there were no more landlocked trout. The spawning season was over. All the spawners should be back in the lake by this time, they reasoned.

For the few days we were to be in the high country we promised to keep watch. And we did. But the spawning time was over. What damage with hand-catching fish was to be done had been done for this season.

There were plenty of fat fish to be caught. And we caught

our share in Fish Hatchery Lake, Pine Island, and the little ponds around these lakes. One or two a meal and a few to take home were all we wanted.

Moreover, we were committed to spend most of our time in the saddle. The scenery committed us — to see that blue sky as a backdrop to the first greens of the timberline summertime and with the huge snowbanks as the feature of the landscape.

The whole land was ours. And we could not mar it by merely looking at it. We left only our footprints, and we took everything else out with us.

How many times over the many decades I've been fishing have I pondered the worth of such devotees to conservation as Dick Goodworth and Guy Bronson! Much of what we enjoy today we owe to men like them.

It Was Not Kentucky Derby Day

I have had some experience with horses. I've been thrown off every family pet in Salt Lake Valley — the ones the kids can climb over all day long, ride bareback, walk under, around, on top of. The last time I was thrown very far was from an old sheepherder's horse in Mill Creek Canyon.

Av Osguthorpe, who owned some of the land there, figured he knew where there was a deer or two — his sheepherder had seen some nice bucks several days before. It was the middle of the buck season. We had waited for the mountain to rid itself of all the footmen who came up for a short hunt during the working lunch-hour — or from daybreak to lunch or from sunset till dark.

Gene Fullmer was with us. At the canyon gate, several miles above the canyon's elbow, we met the sheepherder with the horse I was to take that day. It was a gray with a wild eye. It had been a mustang on the open range. It was broken and trained for use on the range with the sheep herds.

It was an hour before daybreak when we threw saddles on the horses. We wanted to be on top when day broke — so those coming up below us would do the "brushing" for us.

I had a new Weatherby .257, more gun than I ever needed, but Roy Weatherby had made me a special price on it so I bought it. I figured the horse would be accustomed to a gun.

With the gun on my shoulder, slung tight as I have carried a gun many times while on a horse, I slung into the saddle. And I slung right back out of it — by way of what I thought was the moon route. The old gray pitched me higher than any rodeo bronc I've ever seen, and I landed half on my back and full on the rifle. This broke the stock in halves, and right then I was out of a gun.

The three of us taped the broken gun with a splint, and it was workable. I put it in the gun boot. But before I could brush the mud and snow from my legs Av was on his sheep-camp horse on the way up the steepest mountain he could find. When we caught up with Av he had worn the buck out of that horse. He would not throw another rider for a long time.

We had a good hunt that day; killed nothing.

And we killed nothing another day when Av loaned me a horse. An emergency thwarted his hunting plans the night before we were to be on the high mountains east of Salt Lake Valley. He couldn't go, but he offered me his favorite quarterhorse, old Dan. I liked this horse, and accepted his offer because I had involved in the hunt Dr. Y. D. (Enoch) Eskelson, whose time from his medical practice was limited.

I was told to get Dan out of the Highland Drive stables at the Osguthorpe place. It would be in the first stall. The trailer would be there, and the saddle in the tack shop. I knew where the key was — so I was all set.

It was the blackest October night I had every seen, threatening snow and blow, when Enoch and I led the horse from the barn — from the first stall. Time was of the essence so we hurried up the canyon — Enoch had his horse in another trailer.

We saddled up quickly and were soon on our way up center canyon. It was just growing light. The horse stumbled a little — seemed to be unsure of itself on the hard, frozen surface.

Daylight came, and now I wondered why Av Osguthorpe had let old Dan, his beautiful quarterhorse, get so gaunt. The ribs were showing; the horse was thinner than I had ever seen it.

We rode the trail back of the old cabin up to the Lamb's Canyon summit — on a pass between the two canyons. The sun came up and the day grew older. We rode and then waited. Enoch, who had not been around old Dan very much, commented on how thin the horse was.

On the north slope, among the black timbers where the sun never gets until springtime comes, I had trouble keeping the horse from slipping. We tied the horses to a tree and sauntered around to some vantage points when we saw other hunters coming up the canyons below us.

We had lunch and then more riding. Lots of stumbling and slipping on the part of my horse, more than ever before. There were no deer to shoot, just some does and yearling Bambis. Av was at his veterinary office when we returned that night with his horse. He had a broad smile on his face.

"Like old Dan today?" he asked.

I explained that old Dan was pretty shaky, maybe a little too gaunt to be in that kind of action.

Av's grin got greater. Then he explained.

He had moved the horses — put a thoroughbred race horse in Dan's stall and put Dan in the number 3 stall. And he had forgotten to tell me.

I had taken one of the best darned thoroughbreds in the western part of the good old USA on a deer hunt — in the roughest country I had ever hunted.

A far cry from old Churchill Downs!

Dennis and the Bear

Once upon a river trip down the white water of Idaho's Middle Fork of the Salmon River I came around a bend in the river and saw a bear at the river's edge looking for dead fish — or whatever hungry bears look for at the river's edge.

Four of us were running the rapids in two rubber boats, and this was our first day in Impassable Canyon, the last 18 miles of the 108-mile stretch. Dennis McCarthy was in my boat; Norm Tanner was riding with Enoch Eskelson.

We had enjoyed watching the wild animals for several days — the mountain goats with their white furs, the mountain sheep as the lambs frolicked with their ewes. We hadn't, to this point, seen a bear, although we had expected to find one along the river. The gnats were in the high country, and for this reason the wild game animals were at river level. When the gnats and flies come down the wild game animals go higher in the hills. It's a matter of finding comfort in their own habitat.

Dennis and I were the lead boat this day. I knew much about Impassable Canyon and such rapids as Hancock and the brown bear.

Dennis was riding the packs, which we had stowed on the bow of the boat. In this manner we were facing each other. I had the downstream advantage as I was checking my speed in the wild water. Dennis had the best view of where we had been. With the upriver wind this was a desirable position for Dennis to be in.

I spotted the browsing bear over Dennis' shoulder. The bear was busy.

The wind coming up the river was in our favor. Bears are famous for their noses. They can scent you a mile away, especially if you are upwind to them. But they can't see you worth a nickle.

Quickly I had a mischievous thought: I would put Dennis into the bear and give each the surprise of his life — the bear and Dennis. I pulled the bowstring on the spare oar and handed it to Dennis and jokingly asked if he thought he would whip a bear with such a tool. There was just enough bend in the river to make it easy for me to drift at the quarter and head right into the bear — without moving an oar.

"That is a pretty fair weapon," I said, referring to the oar which I had forced upon Dennis. "I think you could give a bear a pretty fair battle with it." Dennis might have thought I was nuts — to hand him a spare oar in the middle of a nice white-water run.

About thirty-five feet from the bear I turned the boat quickly and put Dennis broadside to the shoreline. The bear and Dennis met at the eyeballs. Hair stood on end for each. They were less than two spans of the oar apart.

"Get him!" I yelled to Dennis. The bear bristled in fright. Never have I seen bear's hair stand so upright.

The bruin scampered away, rolling over one log and running smack into a hawberry bush.

Dennis stayed mum. He didn't even get in one swing at the bear. The way the bear took off up the mountain was something to behold. We eddied against the shoreline and watched for several minutes as the bear finally hid in the overbrush on the sidehill.

Enoch and Norm got an excellent view of the bear. They hadn't seen the bruin along the bank until I yelled for Dennis to hit him.

Dennis didn't think it was a good joke. I should have let him enjoy the animal as I did. It would have been a better show that way. But I was being clever and had both Dennis and the bear where I wanted them. You seldom get both parties in this pickle.

Dennis was a sport about it. He did have the oar and could have used it on me.

We have laughed about it over the years. And we have wondered if a fellow could keep a bruin at bay with such a stick.

The Coach and the Clinic

It was 1954 at the Coaching Clinic conducted by Utah State University. The Aggies brought in the most famous of coaches for their annual week of classes.

Not far to the north, Blackfoot River, which flows into Blackfoot Reservoir, was heralded as the nation's best trout water for opening day. The lake fed the river with large spawning cutthroats — whoppers, they were. And everyone in Idaho and north Utah waited for the opening day on the Blackfoot River. I had read about it, and when I went to staff the coaching clinic in Logan I happened to have my fishing gear with me.

Tippy Dye, popular basketball coach at University of Washington in Seattle, was guest lecturer at the clinic, and Tippy and I had talked about a fishing trip during the week he was here. In fact, fishing was one of the baits USU moguls used to lure Tippy to Logan. Let's say a fishing trip was part of the fee.

He had some compatriots in this regard — fishermen like Hy Hunsaker, Steve Belko, Everett Thorpe, Willard Bruce, and a Cache County full of others.

I was unlearned on Blackfoot River matters, so when Tippy and I decided to break out at 3:00 A.M. for the region northward from Logan, I spent the previous evening getting the intelligence reports from everyone I knew. By the time we had Tippy licensed I had enough information, secret data, to last us a week. And we were only going for the morning fishing — prior to Tippy's 2:00 P.M. session.

We found that section of the stream we were told about, and when day really broke we found a hole or two which didn't have a fence line of fishermen. I had been informed that three-inch spoons, brass, was the way to go. I was told to fish them slowly — barely move them across the bottom, casting

*Tippy Dye with a mammoth cutthroat from the
Blackfoot River in southern Idaho.*

upstream and drawing the lure down with the current, fast
enough to keep its action.

All the information I got was correct. We had some big
fish, and we caught some little ones. Fishing was fast and it
was fun. We found enough open water, holes not occupied by
fishermen, to make the day rather sporting.

Limit was ten pounds, and by the time Tippy had three big
ones and a couple of small ones he was weighted out of
action. Tippy had one on that would go about six pounds; the
largest fish he had hooked. No one helped him, and while he
was searching for a place to beach the beast it came undone
and swam away as Tippy groaned.

With our fishing done early, we had a chance to look
around at what others were doing. We thought we had the
best bag of the bunch until we looked upon the catch made by

Joe Datwyler, once from Utah and now from San Francisco. Warren Poole, once from Salt Lake City and now from Soda Springs, had the biggest fish we saw. I guessed it at eight or nine pounds.

We were back at the clinic in good time — had time for lunch. Neither of us changed from our fishing togs, for a reason.

At the two o-clock session, when Tippy Dye was introduced, he came on the auditorium stage dressed as a fisherman, creel, boots and all, dragging a string of nine big fish — our combined catch. All the fishermen in the audience groaned as Tippy tilted the string of fish so all could see — could look upon the lunkers broadside.

He said nothing, took the string of fish to the wings, shook off his boots, unfastened his creel, shed his fishing vest and hat, and then returned with an introductory statement:

"So much for the local fishing. Let's get on with basketball."

About then no one wanted to talk basketball.

I have thought about that morning on the Blackfoot for many years now. I never went back, and for what reason I didn't return, with those whopper fish in mind, I will never know.

Later they treated the lake.

If it was ever as good again I never knew about it.

Sunburned Feet at Pinto Lake

The rains fell hard upon us as we left Mirror Lake and took the Duchesne Creek trail toward Pinto Lake.

Keith Sorensen was an ex-Aggie football player; he had also played on Granite's championship team in 1930. But the pack on his back that day was heavier than most opposing tackles he had encountered on the grid.

Rains made it the heavier as the hours passed on the trail. We were sopped and sagging by the time we got to Pinto Lake. We gathered wood and built a large fire. We were able to warm ourselves on one side at a time and partially dry out our gear.

In 1934 there were no lightweight sleeping bags, nor pocket-sized tents. We had blankets, quilts, and heavy tarpaulins for tentage.

Next morning the sun shone brightly upon us. Not a cloud in the sky. We spread our gear over every small pine, on the steaming grass, on shrubs. Our soggy shoes were left to dry as we took to a raft and went fishing. Fishing was superb, and we caught enough to eat and released the rest.

We paid no heed to the heat of the sun on our bare feet — until six hours later when we felt the burn as we walked toward camp. It was an uncomfortable night as we realized the extent of the burn we had. With flashlights we noticed our feet were blistered. Neither of us could walk next morning. What ugly feet we looked on that day!

Sliding on my buttocks, I was able to go to the lake and get water for cooking. We sterilized some cloths we made from a white shirt. We applied canned milk to the blisters to draw out the heat — someone had told us this was a good remedy for sunburn.

Another day passed. We saw no one. We both crawled to the lake's edge to fish awhile and to get fresh water.

Four days passed before anyone came down the trail. We hollered and they came to us. Kenny Spencer, an old Granite High School chum, was horse-packing through the area. He was a specialist in wildlife and agriculture and was making some studies in the area as part of his schooling. And he was fishing a little during his stops.

Kenny returned to Mirror Lake and sent Forest Service help. Rangers packed us out.

It was not easy to explain why we couldn't go to work for a few days.

Sunburned feet! "That's a new story," Keith's wife-to-be said when Keith said he wouldn't be calling on her for a few days.

Not since then have I taken my shoes off to go fishing. Nor will I!

Elizabeth Lake

Alva Dearden, Rulon Francis and I were looking for a day of fishing on the Uinta Lake north slope. Alva suggested we check with Larry Colton at the Forest Service ranger station to get his advice on where we might go.

Larry was working on his monthly report and had to go into the Elizabeth Lake area for some range survey work. He said if we would wait he would go with us and maybe we could catch a fish in the waters near Elizabeth Lake. Once he had had a nice day fishing there. He had a hunch it could be that good again.

We spread out around the lake to have casting room. The lake was not large. We had to hike to get to it, and I have passed up larger lakes than this because I didn't like their size. Big lakes, big fish, I usually contended.

Right away we were catching fish, two-pound cutthroats. Some of the nicest fish I had seen in any of the Uinta Lakes. They were quality fish, fat on the feed for that altitude.

Rulon stayed on the shallow side and waded deep in the lily pads to fish over a log that was half sunk in front of him. The lake seemed to fall into a deep hole just over the log, and that is where Rulon wanted to be.

From across the lake I watched his rod bend. He muttered something, as if he were snagged. That was Rulon's problem, I figured. He tied his own flies, and if he gave one to a sunken log he would not be much of a loser.

The rest of us kept fishing. Nothing on the top of the lake would indicate Rulon had anything but a log on his line. Rulon, a quiet sort and not one to announce that he had a "fish on," kept a tight line.

Curiously I watched, and I saw his line move a little toward the middle of the lake. Rulon knew he had a big fish on. I was just then beginning to realize what was going on.

I was but 150 yards from him and instantly took in my line and walked his way, stumbling over logs and tundra that had, for hundreds of years, decayed along the lake's edge.

With the sun at my shoulder I could see that silver streak near the surface. It appeared to me that he had what looked like a German U-boat, the one we so often sought during World War II, in tow.

"Looks like a big one," I said in a low tone to Rulon. It was so quiet around Elizabeth Lake we could converse in a whisper from any side of the lake.

"It's a big one," Rulon replied, as he started to move back to shore — at an angle from the sunken log.

He held onto the fish, with a tight line, as if never to alert it — to keep it comfortable. It was a mighty rainbow, and if anything stirred this beauty it would likely churn Elizabeth Lake into a froth.

Alva and Larry worked their way to the side of the lake where Rulon was but never let up on their fly fishing. If Rulon had a big fish, surely that fish had a playmate — or a big brother. Yet all of us wanted to be where, if Rulon needed help, he could have it.

Lily pads are hazards; so are sunken pine trees. But this fish, this day, was opposing one of the best fishermen I knew, and Rulon was using every technique he knew to bring that fish to the shoreline in the most favorable place. It reminded me of a horseman, with the first halter on a fine colt, leading him in the training ring, gently and persuasively, on a demanding tether.

So masterfully done was Rulon's effort that the big fish, hardly awakened to what was in for him, came to the shallows where, once his fight began, he had no thrashing thrust. The fish, which we later weighed at nine and a half pounds, came in side-over into the grass. Rulon, having plenty of rod and line to give the fish in the event of a fight, had backed several yards into the pines.

What a beautiful rainbow trout we admired as it lay, quite peacefully, in the deep grass!

If the lake had been such as would keep a big fish like this for another winter, Rulon, out of admiration for it, might have returned it to the habitat whence it had just been taken. But in bad winters, in the high lakes, the oxygen content becomes so low that big fish, lacking the gill capacity to maintain their body size, die.

So we reasoned.

This was a fish worth wearing on the parlor wall. And perhaps it's still hanging high in the Rulon Francis household in Morgan, Utah.

That was the largest fish I had ever seen taken from a Uinta Lake. And it was done under the most pleasant circumstances.

Don't Overlook That Hunk of Junk

Years ago Luhr Jensen of Hood River, Oregon, one of the nation's top luremakers, sent me a dozen new fishing lures he had stamped out — called the Krocodile.

Luhr was familiar with Utah fishing and had authored a trolling gear called the "Strawberry Special." Its blades were thinnish, and it was often called the willow leaf lure.

In my trade I had field-tested many lures — some for Al Stuart of Al's Goldfish Company (Al actually came West and we both tested his trout-takers on the Provo River, and with some success), and some for Art Helin, the man who invented the Flatfish and made more money on it than has been made on any other sporting goods item.

Luhr's lures worked. I tried them the first day of the season on the Strawberry — back in 1948, as I recall it. As soon as I let out line that morning I was into the fish. I remember filling up so fast that morning that I phoned in an early fishing report from the Carpenter camp (now Charley Woodbury's place) and telling how red hot the Strawberry was on opening day — only to learn later that it was a very poor opening. Maybe I had the lure the lunkers liked.

My friends sometimes called my field testing stuff a lot of "junk," and junk some of it was — at least, in appearance. Ed and Lou Eppinger of Dardevle, for instance, sent me some Kopycats, which were reproductions of the Jensen Krocodile. They were awful-looking hunks of hardware, but they worked.

Some of the junk stayed in the tackle box a long time, and only the curious mind, or the lack of action, brought it to the fishing water.

I enjoyed experimenting with the new stuff. Each time Luhr had a new item, he tried it out on me. He sent me some Krocodile lures once which he had painted blue and then chromed. They were too pretty to fish with — like milady's jewelry. That lure laid in my tackle box for a long time.

One day during the deer hunt, Daryl Shumway and I had tired of hunting in the mountains high above the Strawberry Reservoir. The lake had kept calling to us.

We had bagged one nice buck, hung it to cool, and headed for Charley Woodbury's boat camp. We rented a boat from Charley and went trolling for a couple of hours. Nothing caught fish for us except that blue lure, and we had only one of its kind. But in unhooking a fish I dropped it in the lake. Both of us shed tears when we couldn't retrieve it.

At home that night I phoned Luhr and had him rush me another dozen of the lures. From then on I was sold on a blue-streak Krock, about a quarter-ounce in weight.

I gave so many of those lures away that I ran short of them and then went to several of the stores to buy up their supply. My urgency for the lures must have created bargain-basement panic, for soon there were no such lures to be had.

I guess fishermen talk too much. I do, anyway. When I find a lure I like I tell my friends. I always reasoned that a fish is good for very little until it is caught. That is part true, of course.

I went to New York for a year and a half on a Church call and missed a season at the lake. I came home in mid-October, gave up the deer hunt for some fishing time, and went to Mud Creek Bay, the first place I could get to the lake.

I had just bought a license, but I had not checked what tackle my four fishing partners (my sons) had left me. We have an agreement that anyone's tackle box is available to all the others — family favors. There were a few lures of the blue hue. But I found one I had silvered with a buffer wheel and painted with a single blue streak down it.

On the first cast a large native trout followed the lure to within eight feet of the shoreline. Next cast the fish took it and was soon at my side, flopping on the sloping rocks. Fifteen or so casts later I had to quit. I had eight big fish, casting from the shoreline.

I weighed the fish in Heber; they averaged better than three pounds. I hadn't had a good trout dinner for a long time and I had many mouths to feed, so I kept the catch. But I didn't need excuses to keep a trout; I'm a trout fiend.

The blue-streaked lures taught me a lesson: There might be some odd-ball stuff in the old tackle box for which the fish are waiting.

Since that day when Shumway and Miller discovered the

effectiveness of the blue-silver lure I have gone through every hunk of junk in my keep. Each time I have figured one of them as another winner. And most days, while experimenting, I have come up short in catching fish.

But then, sorting over your stuff and trying it on the trout is often more fun than fighting the repetitions, the boredom, of using the same system, season upon season.

Left on a Sand Bar

I never knew a kinder man than Woody Longhurst of Pocatello, Idaho. Nor a more expert boatman and boat mechanic.

It was my good fortune to get to know Woody well on the friendship cruise between Green River and Moab, down the Green and up the Colorado rivers — about 186 miles.

Ken and Gary Garff had just taken over the area distributorship of the new jet boats, manufactured by Indiana Gear Works. It just happened that Ken took me along as an experienced riverman when Indiana Gear "field-tested" their new jets on the Salmon River. We made that test from Riggins, Idaho, to Salmon City — about 180 miles of upriver white water.

By then I was familiar with the jets, although they were new to the boating public in general. We had five of them on the Green River for demonstrations in handleability, fuel economy, water safety, etc.

The first ten miles from the launching pad at Green River is shallow water, and you must use a great deal of caution in this part of the river. Many boatmen lose their wits here and wind up their prop jobs and soon have broken blades, twisted units, boats which have to be taken from the river or towed the entire distance at great expense and labor. Also there is some partying before takeoff, and some boatmen have a few sheets to the wild winds before they ever take the shift out of neutral gear.

Down river we passed the old Glen Ruby carbon dioxide geyser. (Glen was drilling for oils and gases when he struck carbon dioxide and created one of the state's most colorful cold-water geysers. Glen hadn't wanted to dig there or turn the drillers lose, but the company geologists said that was the spot. Glen later found oil nearby — or gas.)

Then the water got better. The rocky river bottom was covered with sand, and this eliminated much of the propeller damage. We could use a little more throttle from here out, and Woody, in the lead boat, got on plane and we covered the miles.

We stopped at one shoal to remove a stick from the screen which guarded the impeller blades. Two men in a boat, powered by seventy-five horses in the biggest motor of the time, drew alongside and inquired of the jet boat. Woody told them a little about it as we got ready to shove off.

The two men had been drinking. They challenged Woody to a race to Anderson Bottom — about fifty miles down river. Woody wasn't interested. He was testing new boats and had five of them to "mother" like an old hen with her chicks.

The two prop-job cruisers didn't like the turn-down, and when Woody got "on plane" the two men whizzed past us at full open, giving Woody the wake of their turn. Smart alecks, they! They repeated the charge again, and again. Woody was not becoming impatient. He had made his decision. He would not race them.

We talked about the potential of the jet boats. We were heavily loaded in each boat. Also the boats were new, and this was something of a maiden voyage.

On one straight midstream run the two men, having hit old Barleycorn several times an hour, waved Woody on. Way

In a race with a shallow-water jet boat, Green River boaters hit the shallows at high speed and are locked in the sand.

downriver Woody could see some sand waves, and he figured he might try a little jet-boat trick.

He pushed the throttle to the floor (the first jets had floor pedals as in automobiles — foot-feeds). The jet responded and the two challengers accepted the increased speed as a dare.

The boats ran side by side for about a mile. We knew, and so did our adversary at that time, that with his light load he could win a race. But Woody had other plans. Holding close to the shoreline, he forced the prop boat along the tamarack run — not far from the shoreline.

Then it happened. The sand bar started to show above the wind waves. Woody figured at his speed he had to have three inches of water. He knew what depth the prop boat would have to have. We sifted a little sand as we cleared the bar. The other boat dug into the sand so deep that it plowed about six inches of the mud ahead of the prow of the boat.

Woody kept up his speed and returned to the middle of the river. We never again, that day or the next, saw our friends. Woody figured it would take some digging to get out of that sand pit — they would have to lift the boat back up the river.

Those first tests proved what the jet boats could do on rivers, where sand and shallows were the main obstacles.

Woody meant the challengers no harm — just a few hours' inconvenience.

Fishing With Bare Hooks?

Fishermen are great liars; the kind of liars society accepts. Society enjoys listening to a fishing fable, possibly as much as a fisherman favors the telling of it. One of the great stories to come from a piscator is that "the fishing was so good we caught them with bare hooks."

I shall never force that kind of a fable upon anyone. Never has fishing been that good to this angler. But it has been bad enough, on two occasions, that bare hooks were all that would catch 'em.

Once we had a flat tire at Randolph, Utah, and while I was waiting at the service station to get it fixed a state conservation officer, Dave Thomas, came to the station. We had a chat. Thomas and his father were great friends of mine over the years. They were devoted conservation men, and we owe them and their kind much for what they have done to perpetuate our wildlife.

I asked Dave about fishing around Bear Lake, where for the next few days I would be assisting with a youth excursion. He said there was a state-stocked fishing pond in South Eden Canyon and there might be some fish there.

In due time, with my son, Scott, I went to South Eden Canyon. In the clear waters we could see some fat rainbows of about two pounds each — two-year-old fish that had been on a good diet. It was also evident, as Dave had pointed out, that these fish would not survive another low-water winter and they should be caught or they would be wasted. My son Scott, a chip off the old block, is not one to see a fish wasted.

We tried flies, then lures, then nymphs. We caught one or two but were embarrassingly ignored by the others.

How to get them?

I peered through a clump of bushes and watched their feeding habits. They appeared to be standing on their heads, eating off the bottom. I then looked for something in the sandy or muddy bottom of the lake which was causing their head-stand. I found the bait. A small silver bug was digging into the lake bottom, and as the bug moved about it caused a little "dust" to move.

I got out the barest fly hook I had in my pouch. This intrigued them but wouldn't tempt them into striking.

Scott wondered what I was doing when I cast a bare hook into the lake, let it settle to the bottom, and then with tender touch moved it occasionally to stir up the bottom dirt. This attracted the fish and they ate the bare silver hook.

Before Scott got to my side of the lake and adapted his fishing technique to the bare-hook approach, I had my fish and one of his. Knowing what our situation would be when we returned to Bear Lake that afternoon, we took our quota of fish. We had a great fish fry that night — fifteen fish and five loaves.

I never told that story to anyone. Who would believe it?

At Lake Powell on another occasion we found some extremely clear water in Moqui and Knowles canyons. We could see every fish in the shallow waters, and in some of the deeper ones.

I had hooked a lure on some underbrush which had been inundated by the rising waters. I wanted the lure back, so I set out to retrieve it from the bush. I tied a treble hook to my line and tried to hook the lure and pull it from the snag.

While at this tedious task, I aroused the curiosity of some bass and crappie. They swam toward the bare hook and eyed it inquisitively. Suddenly a nice bass bit it, and I soon had the fish on the stringer. Best fish I caught that morning. As soon as I put the hook back in the water another bass of comparable size grabbed it.

I got the hook back, but soon Scott and I were fishing bare hooked. I did not have the desired hooks without borrowing from some of the "baits" in the tackle box. Scott took a surface lure, a Crazy Crawler, and relieved the lure of its treble hooks.

Fishermen in a nearby houseboat, who had fished the canyon waters all day without as much luck as we were having, watched from a distance. They asked what we were using.

Would they believe bare hooks? We spared them that wonderment and told them we were using naked jig flies. We had none of those particular flies to spare. We had a nice string of fish before we left Moqui Canyon later that day.

Two days later in Knowles Canyon I was fishing with Joe Ringhart and Bob Tinnen of Phoenix. Fishing was dead for several hours during the high sun of the day. The lake was so placid you could roll a marble across it. And a smooth lake is often the worst omen for the fisherman.

We drifted into a calm spot in a side canyon and settled down for lunch. We ogled some nice bass in the calm waters. Joe guessed one to be about four pounds. It was interesting to watch the fish, crappie, bass, and blue gills. I tried to jig them into action, but the fish backed off the lures. I used the smallest jig I had, and still there were no takers.

I put on a bare hook and said nothing to my two friends. I

lowered the hook about eye-high to the bass and then gave it a tender wiggle, as a bug would move in the water. One bass came toward it and then backed off; and while the one bass was making something of a study of the unusual "bug," the other darted forth and grabbed it.

I lifted the bass into the boat and showed the two Phoenix fishermen how we Utah anglers do it — with bare hooks.

They were astonished. And so was I!

Then I bare-hooked the other bass, the pensive one.

Joe and Bob had watched the whole operation. It was a study in fish psychology of a sort. You could see, by the action of the fish, their anxiety for the hook and then their quest for it.

"You teased them into it," Bob concluded.

"I have finally seen it done; fish caught on a bare hook," Joe said.

Once before, in my younger days, I had fished for herring (whitefish) on the Weber River. My fly had become so tattered it was little more than a bare hook.

When the last wrapping was gone from the hook, I tried the bare bait, and it took fish as fast as the feathered fly hook. The bare metal resembled something in the herring diet. And I should worry about what that part of the diet was? I had fun afishing, and that was the purpose of my excursion on the river that day.

I shall fish with a bare hook again. May I be so lucky!

The Old Motor Always Started

Bim Meyers had been at the Chesapeake Gun Club at Corinne for many years. Starting his little motor on opening day was a ritual, and everyone took bets on Bim's starting his motor. It was a small motor with a long shank — the kind you need for shallow water when the ice is thick and you have to sway your way to the blind by breaking ice all the way.

Decades ago Bim bet George Earl or Mark Sanders his motor would start in three pulls or less. He had takers.

Next year the losers tried to recoup their bad bets. And so it went for many years.

It was agreed that Bim could not have any practice runs. He had to take the motor as it was, his having promised that no trial runs had been made.

Most of the morning Bim would check the little motor. He would clean the one plug and check the small carburetor — something the size of an eye-dropper.

"You ready?" Bim would ask ceremoniously.

"We're ready," the chorus would chortle.

I remember it well as I stood among those who placed their bets on Bim. There were Harold Willey, Billy Mitchell, George Earl, Dr. Kay Darke, Don Anderson, Bob Carter, Leo Capson, Mark Sanders, Johnny Dooley, Dr. Russell G. Frazier, Del Stoker, Lynn Hansen, George Hansen, Sr. and George Hansen, Jr.

Bim won, second pull!

But the Rod Was Insured

It was on Idaho's Middle Fork of the Salmon River in 1949. Fred Carleson, Cadillac-Pontiac dealer in Salt Lake City, had hired a few of us boatmen to take some of his General Motors friends down the river — on a real adventure outing.

There were four vice-presidents of GM along, and a greater group of outdoor guys I have never known. We had our laughs and our scares, caught fish, watched the wild game animals. It was a trip to remember. In fact, they had us take them down the same river the next year. And they would have gone every year thereafter if it had not been for some changes in their lives about then.

Boatmen on that occasion were Frank Swain, the old master oarsman, Sylvester (Smuss) Allen, Roy Despain, Jack Brennan, Willis Johnson, and this writer.

In Frank's boat were Fred Carleson and Arnold Lenz. Arnold was president of the Pontiac Division of General Motors, the man who put Chevy ahead of Ford and was now in the process of putting Pontiac on the automobile map. Arnold was one of the best sports I ever knew. He was first up in the morning, last to lay himself down to sleep. He was sixty years of age, and sixty to this boatman was an old man. So I tried to treat him tenderly, maybe too much so for his total enjoyment of that wild country.

He liked to lie in his sleeping bag in the morning and watch the stars go away as the light of dawn melted them out of view. And he always wanted to start the day with a warming moose milk, as he called his get-going toddy. Moose milk? That was a little bourbon in warm milk, with a touch of sugar in it. When I made the morning fire to get the coals ready for breakfast, I always set the coffee pot on for those who wanted their Java. And before someone added the coffee, or the egg shells to settle the grounds, I got some hot water for Arnold's moose milk.

And we sat a half hour or more talking about the river and the history of the old Sheepeater Indians who were taken into custody by the militia in the days of the first Indian reservations. Arnold knew quite a bit about Indian lore. He showed me where the Indians had dug their large holes, over which they placed their teepee tents. After seeing these pockmarked places on many river trips, I thought they were placer mine pockets, where someone had placered the sands along the river's edge.

Arnold was such an ardent fisherman that he kept his rod at the ready no matter how dangerous the rapids. He caught a lot of fish just before going into a white water stretch, would fight the fish all the way through the rapids, letting out line as the fish needed it and then bringing the trout to the boat when Frank would eddy-up at the bottom of the hole.

Arnold talked Fred into keeping his rod at the ready. Or maybe Fred was forced into it. Certainly Fred was not the fisherman Arnold was.

Frank must have been fussing with fishing himself when he came to a small falls and went into it sidewise. The boat flipped as the three men leaned away from the hole and tipped the craft. They had to swim for it.

I always followed Frank into the bad spots so that if anything happened I could help. I saw that Arnold and Fred were making their way to shore, and Frank, a seasoned swimmer in such emergencies (he has tipped over on some of the world's toughest rivers), was gathering some of the gear that was still on top of the water. After securing my boat, having recovered a few floating boxes and tackle bags and a hat or two, I went to help Fred and Arnold.

Fred was out of the river and shaking himself down, almost like a water spaniel after it has recovered a redhead duck. Arnold had reached a rock about ten feet from shore and was busy winding in his line. He was all smiles. His glasses were still on his ears, drooping a bit with the heavy water coming from his forehead. He must have thought he was ashore; he stepped down into a deep hole, and I had to retrieve him before he got carried too far into the current.

On shore he continued checking his equipment, and he soon learned he had more line than he started with. He also came out of those rapids with an additional fly rod — Fred's outfit.

Fred walked to where Arnold and Frank were. Other boats came down the river and stopped to see if everything was okay. We sessioned for lunch, and Frank built a large driftwood fire to warm the wet riverrats.

After Arnold had the two rods untangled from their lines,

he handed Fred his fishing equipment.

Fred had done what anyone would do in such an emergency. When you're fighting for your life in white water on a wild river you worry first about getting to shore. Fred did. And as he said, he felt he couldn't swim with a fly rod in his hand. I have tried that. I couldn't manage it either. But Arnold Lenz could and did.

"I had to get rid of it," Fred said, as Arnold gave his rod to him. And in a joking way, Fred added, "Besides, it was insured!"

For the rest of the trip the men kidded Fred about the insurance he carried on his rod and reel. Fred joined in and took the ribbing as only a fisherman can.

I remained on Fred's side. I would have abandoned any fishing stick under the circumstances in which Fred found himself. That's no time to think of fishing rods, insured or not.

Caught on KSL-TV

More fishermen than fish are taken on fishing tackle. Walk through any tackle shop if you want to see an assortment of suckers. And I'm sucker enough to be in some of those sport-shop lines.

If you wanted to catch fish, you could just take a plain old garden worm. Best bait ever known to fish or fisherman. But there's nothing spectacular about a worm. It surely isn't a handsome bait. Worms aren't as gaudy as Flatfish and Triple Teasers, or silver spoons, or Colorado spinners.

As an outdoor writer for more than forty-six years, I got on a lot of the sucker lists. I had many friends in the lure-making business and was what one might call a "field tester." I didn't test fields, by any means — I left that up to the cows and horses. I tested fishing lures — while I was afield.

It seemed I was best known in the mountain trout regions, and anyone who had invented a lure they thought would take trout would send the lure to me for testing.

After World War II, plastics came into being. Inventors went to work to get ahead of the field. After all, Art Helin, with his famed Flatfish, had made more millions than had been made in any other sporting goods item.

On one lure test I was asked by Glen Heiner to check out his "Spin." It was a plastic wiggler, something akin to the Flatfish but in no way infringing upon the patents of any other lure.

In those days I had a daily television show on KSL-TV. I was told it was the first live TV offering on KSL — which meant that I was the first live TV offering between Kansas City and Los Angeles, because KSL was the pioneer in that area.

This matter of firsts isn't too material to the story, however.

I remember when Lennox Murdoch asked me to do this assignment for KSL, I had to go out and buy my first television set — just to note how people on television conducted themselves. It was a nine-inch Emerson. I spent a lot of time in the bathroom, out of everyone's hearing, memorizing certain lines and determining whether I should use a high or a low voice. All that, I learned later, didn't much matter. People were more interested in what we did than what we looked like. (How different that was than it is today, when you have to have your hair done before each appearance and dress in the dandiest duds.)

Lennox Murdoch had titled the program "Hunting and Fishing with Hack Miller." In those first days of TV, and during those field-testing times, Glen Heiner came forth with his "Spim." But how do you demonstrate a wiggling fishing lure on TV?

Well, Glen had a friend at KSL named Rollow Kimball, one of the best engineers in the business and one of the geniuses who erected the KSL station. Rollow and Glen worked out a program whereby they would create a fishing tank, put live fish in it, drag the Spim through the tank, and watch the fish bite at it.

I thought it was ridiculous to think that fish, brought from a hatchery that day, would be eager enough to have action with a moving lure that they would bite at Glen's Spim. But who was I to object? We could have a laugh from it whether it worked or not. After all, Glen and Rollow had worked hard on the program. Two better men I never knew, and I would go along out of courtesy to them.

Also I was responsible on a live show for fifteen minutes. I was taxing my mind to come forth each day with fifteen minutes of prime TV talent. Five days a week, in addition to my full-time beat as Sports Editor of the *Deseret News*.

Incidentally, my bosses at the *News* were happy about this extra exposure. We were in a circulation race against the *Salt Lake Tribune*, and we employed every trick to gain for our product the most attention we could.

And, to make it even better, KSL was paying me a rather respectable fee for so little talent in television.

This tank test for Glen's Spim turned out to be an exciting experiment.

A couple of dozen foot-long trout had been borrowed from Bill Jacklin's state hatchery at Scott Avenue. Bill kept the fish hungry, I learned later, so they would be ravenous when the Spim was worked through the tank. However, we knew that anytime you transport trout from hatchery to wild habitat the fish become dulled from the ride in the oxygen tanks.

As I came to the studio that evening and saw what Glen and Rollow had rigged up, with the blinding kleig lights focused hard upon the fish in the tank, I consoled myself with the thought that whatever happened would be good for the program. We needed a good laugh on "Hunting and Fishing with Hack Miller." We tried never to take ourselves too seriously. So I was prepared for a cut of comedy that night.

I wondered how in the world fish which had been reared in the dull light of the hatchery ponds could adjust their eyes to the powerful flood lights of the TV studio and then, under those lights, became ravenously hungry to pursue Glen's plastic packet.

In preparation, cameramen had a run-through or two, moving the cameras up and down the long tank. They had to be sure they could keep up with the lure once Glen dropped it into the tank and "trolled" it fast enough to give it the action it needed.

I stood ready with all the background data I had gathered on how Glen came by his invention. It was an idea he had had for several years. Plastics permitted him to mold his Spim into the sizes, colors, and shapes he thought the fish preferred.

There was a tongue in every cheek. Alden Richards winked at me as he signalled the start of the program. He was stage director, program director — pretty well everything on the presentation side of the TV setup.

To begin, I gave Glen Heiner a great plug — a beautiful buildup. Meanwhile Rollow stood at one end of the pool with the rod and reel, waiting for the signal for Glen to place the Spim lure in the tank. On signal, Rollow reeled in and the lure was launched. He wiggled it well, and it worked as hard as any lure ever worked. In a split second the fish turned and struck at the lure.

The first trout that smacked it broke loose. Another hit it, and as rainbow trout will, it took to the air and leapt out of the water — onto the floor.

Both Glen and Rollow scrambled to free the fish and return it to the tank. They looked like anything but professional actors as they made for the flailing fish. Cameramen got a lot of hind-pocket pictures as the two men gave up trying to hold face to the cameras.

Once the fish was back in the tank Glen proclaimed, almost in uncontrolled joy, "It worked! It worked!"

Yes, it had worked.

"You've got a winner," Rollow said from the unshown end of the tank.

We had time for several more casts, and each time the fish appeared to be intrigued with Glen's Spim lure as the "big eye" made record of several trolls through the trough.

Glen asked me to field test some of his Spims in the wild waters when next fishing season rolled around. I gave them a try.

One day on the Salt River, while I was fishing with Willard Bruce, Hy Hunsaker, and Everett Thorpe, most everything had failed and I dug into the tackle box and found one of the Heiner Spims.

It was growing dusk and I was working the fast water under a willow tree.

A whopper rainbow gobbled the lure and took off down the river. I was treed in on one side and could only let out line. But the fish didn't stop, and I held the line tight to save it as the fish broke the leader and left me.

Several casts later I landed another Glen would have been proud to have stuffed and displayed on his mantle. Thereafter I was an advocate of Glen's lures and caught many fish on them. But Glen's Spim project faded with time — other lures overshadowed the local fisherman's frolic with his plastics.

Maybe Glen's lures hit the market at the wrong time. His Spim certainly would trick trout, and it should have done more for Glen than it did.

More Time at the Piano

Living beside Mill Creek in those early clear-water, trout-fishing days was a blessing for us kids, even on piano lesson days.

My mother (Mary Jane Guest) was a singer. She had

studied music as a girl at the old Carlisle School at 3900 South and Main Street in Salt Lake City. That was near the old coal yard where Grandpa Guest (Edward F.) and I occasionally went in his half-ton wagon to get a load of coal. As a lad I got to help hitch up old Nellie, the mare, and Buttons, the gelding, to the old Studebaker Wagon for the two-mile ride for coal.

Back to the music. Once weekly I had to report to Lois Walton at West Temple and Thirty-third South, along the railroad track which led to the E. T. Walton Coal and Grain Yard, for my music lesson. Ordinarily I could catch a hay rack down State Street to Thirty-third South and then catch another from State to West Temple, going west. No problem in those days getting a lift on someone's wagon. You never asked for a ride — you just got on.

But I had a better idea. I could fish down Mill Creek to State Street and then at the big hole behind Hustler Flour Mill, down to the Blood Hole, which was fed from the slaughter-yard "juices" at the nearby Archie MacFarland and Sons packing plant. This was always a choice spot because the river trout, even as far away as the Jordan River, were chummed into the area by the flow of feed through the MacFarland faucet.

At the West Temple bridge I would secure my fishing rod while I walked down the dirt road, or took the First West railroad tracks, to the Walton Coal Yard, where Lois, my teacher, waited for me.

After the lesson I would fish back home and usually stay right on the creek until supper time when, after eating, I would be advised to sit at the piano and memorize my next lesson.

I have enjoyed both activities ever since — fishing and fortissimo on the piano. Lois gave me enough music in those two Mill Creek years to provide me with background for many pleasant musical experiences which followed over the years.

And I caught a lot of fish on the way to the Waltons.

A Fishing Lesson From the Golfer

One of Utah's best fishing streams is the Green River below Flaming Gorge damsite. It was particularly good when the water in the reservoir was first impounded. Then the river water was warm enough to sustain a bounteous harvest of rainbows. They grew to good size rapidly, and in a few years there was a ten-pounder caught.

As the lake filled, the water became colder, and this diminished the fishing — they told us the fish could not survive the cold water and eventually made their way downriver where the water was warmer. Sounded reasonable. There had to be some big fish left in the river — upstream or downstream.

I invited Billy Casper to take a float with me one day, a fishing expedition. He brought along young Billy and younger Bobby. Like their daddy, they were ardent about fishing; so much so that young Bobby, wading in the river, almost froze his feet. A cooked lobster never pinked up any better than Bobby's feet did that day on the cold water of the Green River.

My son, Scott, took Billy, Sr., in one boat. I took the Casper kids with me in the other. We launched at the damsite and floated to Little Hole. And we caught many fish, stopping in the best holes to angle for the bigger ones.

Bill caught a five-pounder, and that was a fish worth looking at a second time. The biggest rainbow I had seen come out of the Green River above Little Hole.

I watched Bill bait his hook with a large nightcrawler worm. He used the whole worm. I was using only half a worm, or less. That was the way I was schooled in baiting.

We talked about it. He reasoned that with the many fish in the river (and we could see them in every hole and as we drifted through the deep water at the end of the holes) the fish had to have something natural — a teaser.

So Billy nicked the worm in its head section and let four or five inches of it wiggle with the current. The fish — and we watched some of them — would look at the bait, study it (if fish can do that), and then gobble it up.

It was worth a try, I reasoned.

Bobby and I, with not many good fishing holes left, decided to go for the big one. He wanted to beat Daddy.

Just before we reached the turn at Little Hole, Bobby and I stopped at an eddy below a log which protruded into the river and formed a nice pocket. Not a large fishing hole like the ones we had come through, but large enough to have a fish or two feeding the swift water.

I lagged my gawky bait into the swift water ahead of the tree and let it swirl into the eddy. Whammy! The big one hit it and took off into the white water like a torpedo. The drag was set solid enough that the fish had to turn before it got to the middle of the river.

Bobby was with me all the way, asking to hold the rod. I wasn't about to turn this fish over to an eight-year-old, unskilled kid. Too selfish for that! Bobby ran to the boat and fetched the net and we, together, shorelined the fish. We had big Billy's beauty beat by a full pound, as we learned later when we weighed the two fish.

Bobby extracted a promise from me during that fish fight — I would let him land the next big one.

In the same hole I drifted another Billy Casper long worm and another lunker laid into it. This was a near five-pounder, and I kept my word with Bobby. He took over and fought the fish to submission; and he did a masterful job of it. In fact he brought that fish to shore so skillfully that I shed a little shame for what I had thought of the inexperienced youth a few minutes earlier. This kid was a fisherman.

Before we got to Little Hole we rowed across the river to talk fishing with Scott and Billy, Sr., who had been fishing some choice waters on the south side of the river. Bobby was boiling over with excitement and had to show Daddy his fish and then compare the two. He was convinced he had caught the day's biggest — and that the two we had would outweigh any half dozen they had. They almost did. Bobby had earned the right to talk about that fish for many years. We had pictures to prove all the points he wanted to make.

I learned much from Billy Casper, the golfer, especially about fishing. I guess we get set in our fishing ways — it's like old dogs and new tricks. Never have I fished the Green River since then that I haven't used the Billy Casper long worm.

We were fishing Slide Lake on the Gros Ventre near Jackson Hole one day. Billy was catching some nice cutthroat trout. I was doing poorly, side by side with him and with the sames lures.

He looked at my rig. "Why don't you take off the swivel and tie your line right to the bare lure?" he asked.

I did; and I caught fish.

We discussed it as we drove down the canyon to our motel in Jackson Hole.

"Long time ago I learned that swivels will take some of the natural action from the well-balanced lure. Or maybe it's just a distraction," Bill explained. "But the lure, tied right to the line without all the extra hardware, is far more effective."

After that I followed the Casper rule.

Maybe I have lost some lures because of it. Maybe not. But there's no doubt about it, I have caught more fish on most occasions than others who have been using swivels on like lures and under like fishing conditions.

I Might Have Still Been in Jail

You know how fishermen are. They catch more fish some days than they should.

Jerry Pimm, University of Utah basketball coach, along with Red Stevens, Harry James, and some others, went to Naughton Reservoir in the days when Naughton was famous for its big fish.

We had one boat, but there were many of us. We needed another and Providence petted our backs when we stopped at Cappy Cappellen's place in Kemmerer (he had the sports shops just north of town) to say howdy to Cappy and get the latest data on how fish were being taken at Naughton Reservoir.

Cappy was once a great at Wyoming's football camp. He wound up with some bad leg injuries as a result of the grid grind. But he never lost his feeling for fishermen, his love of life, and his kindness for kids. For many years he organized and promoted kids' football, baseball, and other youth sports at Kemmerer.

Big-hearted buzzard that he was, he offered Jerry, Harry, and me his boat for the day. He hadn't run it much since the previous season, and he confessed it might need some tune-up and plug-cleaning work done. But we were welcome to risk its running if we were daring enough to do it. We dared, and I did spend some time getting it going — clean plugs and a drained carburetor helped.

Somehow Jerry, Harry, and I got into the fish. Maybe it was because we gave up the garden hackle (worms) and turned to casting lures. Red and white Dardevles worked best.

We had a good cooler, and the other fishermen used it occasionally. We were "party" fishing. We were pooling our fish. If Jerry caught more than I did, I would have some of his fish levied against my limit.

Some of us were catching fish and some were not. So we arranged to keep all the nice fish, and we would remain close enough together in three boats that we would all share possession in the event the law checked us. That was allowable, of course. We were all one party, and it was best to keep fish in the right cooling bin.

As it turned out, when Jerry, Harry, and I turned our attention to fishing the other anglers had drifted away. There were many boats on the lake and we could not locate the other two in our party. We knew there were wardens on the lake to check the fish, and with the extra fish we had in our boat and the ones we were netting consistently we would be in trouble if anyone checked us.

Also the other fishermen had told us to keep what we caught because they were not catching any.

For a couple of hours we didn't dare move. We were on a warden watch. We three had not caught a legal limit, but we wanted to be sure, our having traveled so far that day, to take what the law would allow. There were no better-eating fish anywhere than rainbows raised in cold Naughton Reservoir water.

We worried that for some reason the other boats might have been taken to shore and we were left to come to port with more fish than possession limits allowed us.

As the sun started to set, Red Stevens and others came to claim their fish — and maybe some we had caught for them. We were off the hook at last.

"Next time they will carry the cooler," Harry vowed. Jerry and I seconded that motion.

Having a legal limit of your own fish is quite enough.

That Sassy Minah Bird

George Folland said he knew a place where we could catch a fish. In fact, he confessed that he and a fellow named Tom Tucker owned the place. It turned out to be the old Jones Ranch on Yellowstone Creek and Swift Creek, on the south slope of Utah's Uinta Range.

Times have changed since we duded out of there for the Five-Point Lake country in the flippant 'forties. George had built an airstrip, cut a little character into the country. It took out the tilt in the hill. Thirty minutes from the Salt Lake Airport we were standing horse-side in the corral with Tom Tucker and Ike Jensen, veteran packers.

Half an hour later we were solid in the saddle, riding up the Swift Creek trail. The morning sun was still on the day-break slant, and there was a nip of fall in the air. And there was ice on puddles along the trail.

Our destination was some of the better lakes on the Swift Creek drainage. Following Tom's talk about a short cut George and I soon found ourselves nestled against a baldy mountain with a hidden lake all to ourselves.

At first cast a large cutthroat came toward shore to ogle my lure. George caught a couple, and it looked like a quick basket of fourteen-inch trout. But the winds wailed and the fish sulked. We worked hard for a catch of natives, with some brookies added.

I could have set up a homestead at that beautiful site — so far away from the weary world. But our time went fast and delightfully. The day was too soon done. Taking only what trout we could eat (frankly, that is all we could catch), we saddled up and hastened down the trail. It was seven miles to Tucker's cabin.

We had stopped for breakfast at Tucker's place.

He lived alone during that part of the summer. At least, I thought he did. But voices came from a small anteroom which led off the kitchen. It didn't seem there was enough room for anyone else to be there. Curiosity killed me, and Tom sensed I was suffering. So he unveiled his friend, a minah bird, and during breakfast Tom and the bird carried on a conversation.

Tom's hobby was teaching minah birds to talk. Then he had a market for them. They were rare and valuable items.

This bird was exceptionally vocal for lady talk and could whistle a girl down anytime. In fact, Tom got in trouble a couple of times when the bird whistled when it shouldn't have, and Tom had to do some explaining to the lady's escort — or husband, in some cases. The bird was overtrained when it came to pretty ladies. But like Tom confessed, that made the bird more marketable.

I got my comeuppance when I started my conversation with the bird and he shut me up quickly with, "Listen Buddy, I can talk, can you fly?"

We did fly out after we came out of the mountains. The air was thick in the shade of the West Range as George cranked up his Cessna.

"I've got another lake better than that one," Tom teased, as we left his place. "Might even get you a deer this fall if you come out. And I have a horse that will carry the biggest one on the hill.

Tom called it the Rod and Reel Ranch. This was fastest trip to the primitive area I ever took.

It was a shame to take only a day for it when a week of it would have been my choice. But when you're choked for time as I was it's better to have seen Swift Creek for just a few hours than not at all.

And when the leaves are on the turn and the night ice builds on the bucket, there's never a better time to sit in a good saddle.

One Dollar for Gasoline

In whatever way the genes were juggled or the chromosomes were churned around, I must have inherited the fishing fantasy of my father. He was an ardent angler and an honest one — as Isaak Walton once wrote in his tribute to the Honest Angler.

Dad was a fly purist. He wanted his action on top where he could see it. He could make those trout flies dance so the trout could not refrain from hitting them.

He didn't need the silicone ointments, the licorice-flavored sauces, the tapered leaders. He soaked the small catgut of his day, tied on a dropper fly two feet ahead of his trailer fly, and then with unusual skill tricked his trout.

He was standard in his fly selection. He preferred the coachman patterns on the trailer fly and such as the spread hackles (like the Mormon Girl) on the dropper. And he was not such a purist that he would not thread a minnow or a sculpin on his hook or wrap thread around the thorax of a grasshopper on days when these baits bothered the big ones.

I must have cried, as a youngster, every time my father went fishing without me, for when I was seven he bought me my first fly rod, with a two-bit reel and level line. It was a Christmas present — and Dad always told me Santa Claus was a fisherman. Later I came to know how good a fisherman Santa Claus really was.

One day on the Weber River, when the flies were slow at taking fish, Dad suggested I lag a spinner into some of the deep holes. That was the day when we worked the river as a team — he fished the holes with a fly and remained at good distance to do it. He didn't disturb the hole for my spinner fishing as I came along behind him.

Another reason he suggested the spinner treatment for me might have been my bad luck in popping the flies off my line on my back casts. I was losing a lot of flies, and Dad paid a nickel apiece for flies in those days — and a nickel would buy a loaf and a half of bread.

We fished for many years this way when I thought I could lure some of the lunkers from beneath the tree stumps or willowed banks — usually in the swift waters.

Dad always caught the most fish. Fly fishermen usually do when the surface feed is on. But I got the gluts — those regal rainbows in the eddies and the bulky and belligerent browns on the far sides of the fast water — those that went for the minnow hatch or the bullheads. I was tutored by a master, and as the years passed I found I could take trout from just about any lake or stream and most every day I went afield. Many times some of my pals could go with Dad and me, and I soon had some fishing pals who could take fish from any good water.

One day two Utah Aggie football players, with whom I had grown up, went with me to the Provo River. Keith Sorensen and Turk Jackson had been on the Granite High state championship football team in 1930 and had been lured to Logan's camp by Coach Dick Romney. In the summers they came back to the Granite area to work, and we had some fishing time together. I have never contended Utah Aggie fishermen were any better than Utes or Cougars, but these two men could take trout with the best of them.

We started fishing near the old Hailstone Junction, where once there was a saw mill and uproad a bit there was the Hailstone (Murdoch) power station which churned out electrical power from the millrace that came off the mountain. The millrace ran to the river through what we knew then as the Davis Ranch.

The dynamos in the Murdoch plant were always humming, and sometimes we checked in to talk to the powermen and find out how the fishing had been and to pay the twenty-five-cent fee the Davises charged for parking in their place for the day. We usually fished the spillway and then, once on the river, fished upstream through the Davis, North, and Berg Ranches. We had friends at all three places.

Trout were feeding the surface that day, and in Dad's two-fly style I caught trout quickly and soon had a creel lined with nice fish — some weighing in the two-pound class. Our limit was thirty in those days, and we usually took a limit if we could catch and carry them, because in depression years there were not only hungry folks at home but the neighbors appreciated any trout a fisherman could spare.

Keith and Turk had gone upstream ahead of me. I was quite alone when I noticed a dapperly-dressed fisherman coming downstream in the hole ahead of me. I watched him fish. He was a novice, and to me that meant he was not going to make much motion in our fishing. Fish didn't pay much attention to novices in those days.

In a few minutes the fisherman and I were sitting on a log talking about fishing.

A gentle fellow he was, eager to be a skilled angler. But he had problems. He caught so few fish that he could not convince his wife he was really out trouting in the time he was away from home. She suspected he might have been using trouting matters as an escape from his marital responsibilities. He had taken only a few fish home in his day — so few that his wife, he said, thought he had bought them at the fish hatchery.

My creel was hanging heavy on my shoulder. Tails of a couple of large fish were showing at the top of the creel. The man sitting with me on the log kept eyeing my basket. He had a creel which appeared to me never to have carried a fish. It was surely not "stunk up" as good fishermen's creels always were. It looked so store-bought and new.

He finally asked if he could see my fish. Of course he could, and I unfastened the creel's lid. You could have knocked his eyeballs off with a stick as he gazed upon my catch — and I had just started.

I had to chuckle, mostly in sympathy, as he explained that he had taken up fishing to get some away-from-his-wife time and had done so poorly at it he remained a suspect each time he went home. He had been given an ultimatum by his lady that if he didn't bring home fish she was going to peddle his fishing outfit. He laughed the harder when he mentioned that she was going to sell it to her brother at a reduced price — and I chuckled when I realized this new friend of mine didn't care much for her brother.

"Would you sell me some of your fish?" he asked abruptly. He knew I understood his plight.

"I've never sold a fish in my life," I told him. I never knew anyone who wanted fish enough to buy them — especially when it seemed there were plenty in the river and would always be enough to go around. And I never knew until that day that there were people who could not catch fish.

I pondered his proposal. I couldn't sell a fish; I would give him some. I got them from the river; there were more where they came from. Selling them would be going too far, and I told him so.

My basket was already heavy with fish and I had the rest of a good day ahead of me. He could have all of them if he really wanted them. He accepted half a dozen nice trout and I pulled some fresh willow leaves to place under them in his creel.

Quick as a wink he tucked a dollar bill in my shirt pocket. I objected.

He said he was not paying me for the fish — just helping pay for some gas for my next fishing trip.

A whole dollar — and how many times I could not go fishing because we couldn't rake up forty or fifty cents to buy enough gas to get there — at seven cents a gallon!

I guess I accepted his latter proposal, because I kept the dollar. He needed the fish; we needed the gas. Favor for favor. No sale, really.

I consoled my sporting feelings in contemplating his joy when he walked in to his lady this night and spread those trout upon the sink board. And how he thwarted his brother-in-law's move to get his fishing outfit for a pittance.

The old Whitestar Service Station in south Salt Lake City was wholesaling gasoline at fifteen gallons for the dollar. That tank and a half of gas would buy us four more fishing trips — if we turned off the ignition and coasted down all the hills.

For many years thereafter I watched along the streams to see if I could locate that friendly fellow.

I was forever curious to know if he ever became expert enough at fishing to keep his wife from whining — or if his antagonistic brother-in-law ever lured his fishing stick from him.

Deer in the Yard

Maybe this story isn't entirely true, but it was told to me as a hand-on-the-Good-Book happenstance.

As hunters will, they make an event out of the deer hunt. Some have trailers; some live in tents. Some have fancy cabins.

Several Cache County sportsmen with access to a cabin in Logan Canyon spent an enjoyable evening around the campfire talking, possibly about the opening of the deer hunt next morning. They found themselves in no hurry to hit the sack. This was their annual outing. They stayed up late — and got up late the next morning. No one was in the mood to brave the deep snow that had fallen during the night. There were plenty of days to hunt.

After stretching and putting the kettle on the front burner, one of the pajama-clad hunters went to the kitchen window, wiped the steam from the glass, and peered out. There on the lawn, looking startled, was a nice buck.

The hunter hurried for his firing piece. He looked out of the window to determine which was the best way to attack this problem, when he noticed another buck standing on the lawn and a third barely peeking out of the trees.

As the story goes, and I wrote a column about it, these

hunters had their deer down before they had their pajamas off.

I don't know if they shot out of the kitchen window or not — maybe they shot it out rather than disturb the deer.

But that is the story.

Some say the hunters went back to bed to grab a few more winks before they ever considered dressing out their deer.

Not a bad story. It could happen. Maybe it did.